PLAN ON BREAKING THROUGH

CUSTOMER-BASED STRATEGIC PLANNING FOR SELLERS

FRANK HURTTE

About River Heights Consulting and River Heights Consulting Press:

River Heights Consulting is a boutique consulting practice dedicated to the improvement of knowledge-based distributors and their supply-partners. Founded by Frank Hurtte in 2005, River Heights Consulting has worked with organizations on five continents and published over 500 articles on the topics critical to the wholesale distribution industry.

River Heights Consulting also sponsors The Distributor Channel Blog which has hosted over 100,000 viewers.

River Heights Consulting

SINCE 2005

Table of Contents

Forward

I know what you're thinking, does the world *really* need another book about sales planning? I have to admit, I struggled with the question when Frank first told me about this book. Planning is fundamental in any business. It also happens to be a huge issue for most salespeople. I also questioned if strategic planning principles truly apply to individual accounts. Reading through the early manuscript, the answer to both questions became abundantly clear. The world of sales *needs* this book.

Most salespeople have become tactical and reactionary in their sales approach. In my work with building sales processes through Customer Relationship Management, one of the biggest issues I see comes via short sighted sales efforts. For some, selling time is devoted to identifying an opportunity and quickly providing a quote resulting in a hastily prepared generic proposal. With others, the sales effort is focused on reactively waiting for a customer to have an issue then quickly, sometimes blindly, responding to the emergency. Each iteration is viewed as a standalone interaction without thinking of advancing the salesperson's company or position with the account. Where's the strategy here?

This book is not about the typical business or distributor sales planning. Instead, it guides the sales professional through the process of strategically moving a customer relationship forward. Note, I said "a" customer relationship, as in the singular. Everyone understands a generic strategic plan will not work for your organization. Yet sellers employ a generic plan to grow their accounts without regard to specific customer situations. Hurtte drives home the point that sellers must approach each customer differently.

Creating a customized plan is a time investment. The author equips the salesperson with the tools required to determine the best chance of success. Thinking about it the whole subject mirrors a thought I recently shared on the SalesProcess360 Blog:

"Quoting takes time and money, and there are times when more quotes do not lead to more sales. Imagine that a company has requested quotes from you 20 times in the past six months, but hasn't purchased from you once. If you continue to generate quotes for this company without first trying to figure out why you're losing, you'll be wasting time and money...."

In most organizations, and certainly within the ranks of distributors, the typical sales professional has more potential selling opportunities than they have time. Extending this thought further, some of these prospects will never materialize for your company. Why? Not every potential customer needs your services or matches your organizational values. Some have such solid relationships with competitors, meaning success just won't happen in your lifetime.

This book outlines how success comes by way of understanding the how to pursue the right customers and opportunities. Sadly, perhaps ironically, even experienced sales professionals often lack the skills and objectivity to truly understand what Hurtte calls "where you stand" at the account. This book breaks down the process and equips salespeople with tools for making the right decisions.

Salespeople who develop a separate strategy for each of their major accounts tend to offer up better solutions and position themselves for long term, sustainable success. Moreover, salespeople who evaluate their accounts based on potential for success invest their time more wisely. Finally, salespeople, who "follow the money" position themselves differently with their customers.

What's more, this book is an easy read. Frank's masterful story telling style combined with discussion points at the end of each chapter turns this effort into a valuable coaching tool for sales managers and a timely exercise for the sales professional looking to up their game. The lessons outlined will improve your sales numbers and impact your sales process. In my opinion, a sales process is the only way for an organization to drive long term success with important revenue generating customers.

In the long haul, organizations who become their customers' business ally and competitive advantage prosper through the ebb and flow of business climates. In my mind, no sales manager, business owner or sales professional can overlook this strategic advantage. Now truly is the time to apply strategic planning principles to accounts.

Brian Gardner, Founder of SalesProcess360

Acknowledgements and True Confessions

First, I would like to thank my many clients and readers of The Distributor Channel Blog who have provided me the opportunity to spend time with salespeople, sales managers, heads of sales efforts and countless other front line sales types who provided me with the opportunity to watch selling in progress.

Amongst the hundreds if not thousands of sellers I have witnessed in action, all but a miniscule fraction were willing to share thoughts and insights. These folks were warm, friendly and open to discussing ideas for improving the lot of sellers in general. The best of the best, seemed almost driven to helping further the science of selling. My thanks to these great folks.

I would like to especially thank Brian Gardner of SalesProcess360 for his encouragement and occasional emails and other nudges to get this thing finished.

Now for the True Confessions...

Number One: I started selling in my father's distribution business at the ripe old age of 14, worked my way through college selling encyclopedias and have just surpassed the four decade mark in the "real world" of distributor sales.

Over all of these years, the world of selling has shifted, morphed and reformed. The only thing remaining constant is the hours in a day and the human condition. I believe the rest is up to the innovations of each new generation of sellers.

Number Two: This book isn't perfect. I opted for "light editing" over the strict guidelines of a professional editor. This may have been a dumb idea, but I wanted to make this as personal as possible; my personality, flaws and all. If you find a passage with poor grammar and can't understand it, call me. I will spend time explaining exactly what I meant.

Number Three: I make reference to Thomas Jefferson several times throughout the book. My apologies to those of you not familiar with U.S. History. Thomas Jefferson was the third President of the United States and principle author of the American Declaration of Independence. He coined the phrase, "All men are created equal..." This did not apply to customers back in 1801 when Jefferson became President and it's even more so today. It took me close to seven years to learn this valuable lesson.

Number Four: There are a few places where I get preachy. The ideas contained here work with almost any account. They will work with all of your accounts. But, you don't have time to make them with every account on your customer list at the same time. Again, in the early stages of my career, I missed this point. It cost me time, money and probably set my professional life back a few years. If I get on my soap box too much, just chalk it up to a person who is still passionate about selling (after all these years).

Introduction to Account-based Strategic Planning

During recent years, I have assisted dozens of organizations in creating a simple and workable strategic plan. Along the way, I have witnessed some flowery documents; content rich in filler but lacking anything killer. I prefer simple, straightforward copy with lots of action, metrics and laser-focused documentation. My clients have discovered a powerful bullet point outline trumps a 50-page cornucopia of buzz words. The right document turns into an ongoing guidepost; focusing the minds and long-term direction of the company. Each time you make a tactical decision, the broad ranging strategic plan serves as a directional North Star.

Experience dictates, companies with an effective strategic plan prove more successful than those who simply go with the flow. While I can name a few pretty successful organizations choosing not to develop a plan, I have a deep seated belief that a working plan increases the odds for maximizing long-range success.

After reviewing "strat plans" from hundreds of businesses, I see a breakdown. Even though the leadership team had ideas about market conditions which are exploitable, technologies to be capitalized, and competitors easily replaced, behaviors needed from their sales teams remained a major obstacle.

Should Salespeople have Strategic Plans?

Returning to my hotel from a very long day spent in a strategic planning session, I had an epiphany. Many of the very best salespeople operate their territories as if their customer list was an independent businesses; albeit a stand-alone enterprise flying in close formation with the rest of the mother company. Most sales managers live with, perhaps even encourage, a certain level of controlled entrepreneurial spirit out in the field.

Being totally spent from the day of planning, the "entrepreneurial thing" rattled in my subconscious mind. Might it be possible to push a strategic planning process to those closest to the customer? During the next few weeks, I talked to a collection of the sellers recognized as top performers in their companies and industries. A fundamental difference in the way they thought about customers emerged. Even though individual sales call activities were similar to their contemporaries, application acumen, product skills and problem solving were about the same. They consistently outperformed the rest of the pack. Why? Because, they thought about accounts with a long-range strategy.

I discovered most salespeople with five or more years of experience are proficient in the transactional components of selling. They connect with their customers personally and professionally. Because they understand product and technology issues of the customer, the salesperson's business increases. At first glance, one would say they are headed down the road to success. But with time, acceleration of growth slows, plateaus are hit, and the seller's overall development is hampered.

Even with this "journeyman" experience, the average seller treats each customer interaction as a reactive event. It's a never-ending carousel ride where one identifies issues, solves problems, and the process repeats with no end in mind. Any vision of account development is short term; with a good many struggling to define account development at all. Sales skill improvement comes tied to the seller's ability to accelerate the rotational speed of their selling merry-go-round. It's a reactional game.

Sales managers complain their teams lack the ability to properly utilize all the resources available to them. Business level conversations with customer management are seldom carried out, and when they exist at all, the content rarely moves things forward. Selling time, resources and organizational energy are wasted on the wrong accounts or focused on the right account, at the wrong time.

What might happen if we applied the principles of strategic planning to a sales team's best accounts? As simple as it sounds on the surface, when salespeople apply the same processes found in their parent company's strategic plan, customer-centric thinking improves. Sales effort shifts from a string of single events to a consequentially planned maneuver for sales growth, competitive position and mutually beneficial partnership.

Building an Account-oriented Strategic Plan
We could toss out a bunch of consultant speak, but cutting to the chase, the strategic plan revolves around an understanding of current position and exploring future options with the goal of impacting the future. Before moving ahead, those responsible for the plan devote a great deal of time completing a SWOT analysis. We painstakingly identify strengths, weaknesses, opportunities and threats with as much objectivity as possible. Even though the whole concept sounds relatively straight forward, many organizations struggle because today's small issues become emotional barriers standing in the way of longer-range thinking.

Salespeople planning for long-range success face even more emotional baggage. By its very nature, selling is a high contact and visceral game. This emotional aspect calls for management coaching and insistence on incremental steps to creating a meaningful plan.

To facilitate incremental thinking and provide the right level of coaching, I break the strategic plan into progressively important phases. Let's think about the significance of each of them as applied to a substantive account.

Where do you stand at the Account? Wouldn't it make good sense to pause for short while and ponder the question: What does the customer think of our organization? Or better yet, how do they see me in the context of a supplier? Do they respect my company, or are we just another in a long litany of guys the customer buys from? Is our organization noted for "dirty deeds done dirt cheap" pricing, or are we a value- producing machine standing ready to be called upon?

These points are sometimes painful to ponder. In what Jonathan Bein of Real Results Marketing refers to as the Lake Wobegon Effect, everyone thinks of their organization as above average and the veritable deal of the century. Maybe some accounts think of you that way. But in our account-based planning, we've got to understand how this customer thinks of us today.

What do you know about the Account? Strangely, sales types gloss over account knowledge. Oh, they have general ideas as to the products and services provided, but they lack deep understanding of the customer's business interworking. Even though most swear to be "solution providing" sellers, they lack details on the customer's labor rates, business costs and market sweet spot.

Taking an inventory of knowledge around an accounts business situation provides coaching points for the management team and the ability to call in outside assistance. Thinking critically on this topic gives the salesperson future direction in areas worthy of exploration.

What level of Prioritization does an Account Justify? Thomas Jefferson wrote, "All men are created equal...", but trust me, all accounts are not created equally. We don't have time to create a strategic plan for every account on our list. And universal, one-size-fits-all plans don't pack the same power. Somewhere along the way, we must objectively determine if an account fits the right criteria to justify our efforts.

Again, setting prioritization allows management to ask coaching questions and provide an outside opinion on an account-by-account basis. Good salespeople appear universally optimistic; sometimes to their own detriment. Benchmarking data, previous experience with similar accounts and other guidance help expand the chances of success.

How do you think about Account Opportunities? Sticking with our Thomas Jefferson analogy, some accounts are easier to convert than others, some require high activity levels for a short duration and others require a longer continuum but less intense time investment. As they say here in Iowa, some are low hanging fruit and just require the picking. Time pressures may prohibit working two time intense opportunities simultaneously.

Without sounding overly stereotypical, salespeople have a habit of underestimating the time required to achieve selling objectives. With "too many balls in the air," the chances of costly errors increase. Opportunities are lost, and customer confidence dwindles. Some strategic thought allows better scheduling and execution of plans.

Are you following the Money at your Account? The truth is most salespeople follow technology, customer application needs and pursue friendly contacts. Salespeople rarely follow the funds. I can't help but wonder if a lot of salespeople actually feel they cheapen their work through the exchange of money. How many times you have heard a salesperson lament: "The proposal was perfect. The product was everything the customer wanted. We were the best supplier on the planet. But, the customer didn't have any funding?"

Call me mercenary, but I believe today's sales team must consider the finances. Just evaluate the cost of building a decent proposal. Days of time spent pulling information together, gathering details from suppliers and crafting the whole thing into a presentation can run into the thousands of dollars for selling team. Understanding who controls the purse strings (and if the purse has anything in it) is critically important.

Who do you know at the Account? Thinking more about the money, why do so few sellers take the time to build relationships with high- level management types at our accounts? I regularly get calls to jump in and help "save an account" because somewhere along the way, the salesperson has never built a relationship with the guy who writes the checks.

Account top brass call the shots. Regardless of what your technical guy or project manager tells you, if Mr. Big says to switch the business, you're done. Sales managers lament the situation but lack the tools to understand if calling on Mr. Big is a nod in the hall or a meaningful discussion of the value provided by your company.

What Value do/can you bring to the Account? Enough about your great service, fast delivery and wonderfully trained inside sales people. Let's get down to some meaty stuff. Directly and specifically, what can you do for this account? This isn't part of the boilerplate on your website. Nor is it a list of nebulous goodies. Instead, precisely how can you help this single account make more money, gain market share, boost their efficiency or improve their productivity? Name names, give figures, cite recent examples.

Most sellers leave it to the customer to connect the value dots. No salesperson has the time to do it for every account. But they do have time to make the effort at a select list of accounts. If they take the time to follow the previous steps, they know which ones to focus on.

Still don't believe me? Let's put the concept to a test.
You may be skimming over these past couple and nodding in agreement. But deep down, you're thinking, "My sales team is already doing this. They're professional, they're smart, and (just like the children of Lake Wobegon) they're all above average. This strategic planning thing is for everybody else."

The first chapter of this book contains a simple test. In a matter of five minutes, you will start to have a feel for the depth and quality of your plan. Whether you are a seasoned salesperson, a sales manager or the leader of a company, taking an objective look at the next chapter will steer your thoughts.

Part One
How Strategic Are your Sales People?
A three question test.

Just ask any salesperson if they work a strategic plan focused on developing their accounts and I will bet you a brand new nickel they will answer with a resounding, yes. Most will back up their story with details on how they are exploring new opportunities, meeting new contacts, improving their business relationships and mega-doses of other good stuff. No doubt, you will start nodding along. Perhaps, you will be completely sold. Salespeople can be optimistically convincing. I like this quality in a seller.

But sometimes, I suffer buyer's remorse. A few weeks after being "sold" on a salesperson's strategic plan, I asked for something relatively simple; actually a couple of things. Sales projection for a new product, insight on the customer's market position and thoughts on whether an OEM uses spare parts as a profit center. My inquiry could have been just about anything, but the point is, the answer wasn't very satisfying. I needed to be resold... Tell me again about your strategic plan?

Have you ever found yourself in this position? If so, don't feel like you are the only one. Sales managers from around the country candidly share their concerns: their team doesn't plan enough. More specifically, they rarely plan in a long-term strategic way. Apparently, these managers suffer from buyer's remorse, too.

If you happen to be a salesperson reading this, you may be wondering about your own planning process. Perhaps, you are asking yourself these questions. Is reacting to customer requests as good as it gets in sales? How do I become more important to my customers? Why must I always chase customer opportunities, as opposed to having a stable of loyal customers who ask me to sit down as a co-equal at their planning sessions?

Over the course of River Heights Consulting's work with sales groups from dozens of distributors and manufacturers, we have developed a three question test for strategic planning at the account level. And because it's a beautiful day here on the high bluffs of the Mighty Mississippi, I am going to share this test with you.

Question One: Tell me the plan for your next sales call at XYZ Company (which is in the salesperson's top 5 accounts). I want to know as much detail as possible. Who are you going to talk to? What are you going to talk about? Who else from our organization will be involved?

For most sellers this is easy. They have a strong idea of the next selling opportunity, what needs to be handled and often have plans for some sales ally or product specialist to be part of the mix. The answer and information will smoothly flow off the seller's tongue. Perfect now move the next question.

Question Two: Thinking about this same account, what will you be doing on a sales call in 30 days? Again, give me as many specifics as possible.

If the salesperson has even a rudimentary plan, they will demonstrate how the first call is tied to this next customer interaction. Or, you may discover the seller is working on multiple customer issues and this interaction some 30 days forward is another well thought out standalone event. In any event it will provide perception to short term planning at the account.

Experience dictates experienced proactive salespeople have a handle on their strategy a month out. Even the sales guy who merely reacts to customer emergencies and various product requests can bluff their way through this discussion.

Question Three: Looking again at this same account, what do you feel you will be working on in 120 days?

Plans for activities four months forth are an early litmus test to strategic sales planning. One would expect even the most rudimentary strategic plan for an account to extend into the next quarter. Saying this, most salespeople's response provides definite clues to their lack of planning.

What would a good answer be? Well, for one thing, a sign of a plan would be thoughts on expanding the business. A good response might go something like this:

"By the end of the calendar quarter we hope to position ourselves with the field service team of the customer. We want to gather information on the number of emergency field trips taken and the cash outlay for each of these trips. This will enable us to present our plans for a remote access system to management complete with financial data."

Or the conversation might look like this:

"We want to strengthen our position with the customer by eliminating small vendors. Over the next few months I will be identifying products for conversion and presenting them to our current internal coach. I suspect that in four months we will have identified a hit list and be ready to ask management to switch the business to our team."

How do you or your team begin to think more strategically?
To start we must begin working to develop detailed strategic plans for the seller's top five or ten accounts (not all). Experience shows, the time required to carry out the exercise on every account creates an emotional overload; an environment where no real planning takes place. Further, each strategic plan must be customized and focused on the specific issues of a single customer relationship.

For those who hope to apply this process to every account on their 200-plus account list; a word of caution. Don't! Trust me, developing the practice for your very top performing accounts strengthens your natural tendencies to think long-range. Many of the practices will spill over into daily behavior with time. As a person who has assisted many companies developing organization wide strategic plans, I continually push my clients to focus in on the five to ten strategic initiatives with the greatest potential return. For the typical seller, focusing extra energy on the accounts at the top of their account list truly does provide the greatest potential return.

As we move forward, we will explore the individualized steps required to build a real strategic plan for our accounts. Sliding into the next chapter, we will explore the importance of understanding our current position at the account.

Points to ponder:

If you are a salesperson and tested yourself:

- How would you rate your personal strategic plan?

- Do you have plans to address longer term competitive issues at your top accounts?

- How often do you step back and think about your position at your best customers in one or two years?

If you are a sales manager thinking about your team:

- How would you rate your team?

- Do you have a few salespeople who are more forward thinking than others?

- Do you see a link between longer range thinking and growth success?

- Take a few moments to rank your team from best long term and strategic and those with little long range vision.

Part Two
Knowing where you stand

The gnarly voiced, wizened old singer on a scratchy vintage 78 rpm disc said something like this:
"If you want to get from here to Nashville son, you better know where here is." I believe this advice applies to the first step in a seller's strategic account plan.

Where are we with the account?
As reasonable and basic as the question sounds, many sellers refuse to realistically understand their importance with an account. Most struggle with understanding their individual strengths, and almost none face up to professional vulnerabilities.   Repeatedly salespeople tell me, "I get the 'lion's share' of the business at this account." Yet, when I visit the account on coaching or target evaluation calls, I see pallet loads of competitive product coming in the door. Deeper study indicates whole technology segments supplied to the customer by the guy down the street.   We see a long list of competitive sales guys signed in at the reception desk; often calling on people the seller doesn't know.

How do we know where we stand as a supplier? Are we viewed as an important extension of the customer's organization? Are we seen as the guy who provides a widget so complex that dealing with us justifies the pain of our idiosyncrasies? Are we one of many low cost vendors, or are we important for some real reason?

Let me restate the obvious. We've got to understand where we stand with the customer in order to build a plan that extends anywhere past next Tuesday's drop by sales call.

I am perplexed as to why sellers don't simply ask, "Where do we line up with your organization as a solution provider?" I believe the real reason many don't is fear. Sometimes, the truth smarts. What happens if the customer responds with a negative answer? Often, sellers ask the question of the wrong person. Your company may be "numero uno" with the one guy in maintenance, but viewed as a necessary evil by plant management. Other times, the evil ones in the purchasing group deliver misinformation to sellers to satisfy their own price-driven agenda. Understanding the real answer involves interacting with a number of people at the account. To emphasize an important point, financially focused management types must be on the list.

In addition to simply asking, here are a half dozen sure-fired ways to understand your position:

1) Do a plant tour/facility tour with an eye for competitive products in use. If you see applications using the products provided by a competitor, make it a point to understand why they were selected over a solution provided by your company.

2) If your customer maintains a store room or parts crib, look at products kept in stock alongside those you are providing.

3) Drop by the customer's receiving area to check on service levels. While there, look for shipments coming in from your competitors.

4) Analyze your sales to the customer. Look for gaps in purchases. Think about what other products might be used along with those you are selling the customer.

5) Ask your key contacts who else is a supplier and what they like about their service.

6) Ask someone, and be prepared to listen, not argue the point.

None of this tells you precisely where you stand with the customer, but it will give you a better idea of the competitive landscape in which you operate. In addition, it will take you to the point of being able to rank your position against competitors at strategically important customers. Your plan will make use of this information to determine how to approach the customer.

Percentage of the Customer Spend.
Understanding your "wallet share" at the customer often provides insight to your position at the customer. One of the best sources for this information could come by way of the purchasing department. As outlined previously, procurement professionals are trained to provide sellers with misleading information around sales numbers. However, with a little planning one might derive information.

The first approach involves asking about the overall budget. For instance, if you sell your products into the maintenance department of a larger organization, why not ask the maintenance manager about their total budget? As a follow-up ask if they break out parts versus labor and other expenses.

Benchmarking your customer against known accounts works to develop a feel for customer spend share. Select another account from the same industry and contrast sales to each account. This works best when sales of various product types are compared in a side-by-side manner. Factor in the number of employees to build a scale to adjust for size of the companies.

Many industry associations accumulate and publish benchmarking data which can again provide a picture of the approximate purchases of various types of accounts. For instance, Electrical Wholesaling Magazine publishes an annual market guide which lists approximate purchases per employee for a number of business sectors. From their information, one can deduce that electrical contractors purchase just over $49,000 per employee or $71,000 per electrician employed. Similar numbers are published for commercial institutions, utilities, Industrial MRO accounts, automation accounts and mining companies. Are any of these numbers 100% accurate? No, but they will provide insight into the approximate spend for the customer.

Competitive Positioning and Customer Wallet Share aren't the Only Issues
We steered clear of point blank asking someone at the customer where we stand. While competitive position provides many clues, what happens if the customer isn't really satisfied with any of their suppliers? This

occurs more often than suspected. There are other clues to your position at the customer.

Is your company embedded into the customer's processes? For instance, if your organization handles some regulatory/reporting tasks for the customer, reporting back with final government approvals or files, you are embedded. If your organization handles some bit of inventory maintenance or manages the spare parts orders going to the customer's customer, you are embedded.

In each instance stated above, the customer has shown a level of trust in your company's work. The greater the responsibility handed off to you, the more highly regarded are your efforts. When suppliers have become an integral portion of the customer's work flow, they are difficult to replace. Being difficult to replace is important.

Are you asked to participate in process improvement, Kaizen or similar business improvement events? Spots at these meetings are generally reserved for top level suppliers; those held in high regard and noted as important. While the practice of "Kaizens" are not universally followed, many of our customers actively pursue business improvement. Asking whether the events even exists differentiate you from others. Hearing why you were not asked to participate may give you a clue as to your status.

During the previous few paragraphs we made positive assumptions. Now let's turn the tables. If you are involved in any of the embedded process or organizational improvement activities of your customer, are competitors involved as well? You may need to do further research. Perhaps you are viewed as the "ideal" provider of just a segment of your customer's needs. For example, many electrical distributors also sell electrical automation products. Are you viewed as the expert on "electrical commodities" and someone else totally engaged in the automation sale? The point is: With many distributors branching into new technologies, you may find yourself excluded from great potential business.

In a worst case scenario, you may discover, the competitor is far more embedded with the customer and holds a more solid position than your organization. It's not a pretty picture. But, it is far better to realize your predicament and begin the road to creating a strategy for building on your current place in the competitive landscape than to enjoy ignorant bliss.

Looking forward...
Understanding your position is only the first piece of the puzzle. As sellers, we strive to improve our position. Without a detailed view of the inner workings of the customer, any plans for growing our business is only a blind shot in the dark.

Points to ponder:

- Who are the competitors at your account? How do you rank against them? Which are weak and vulnerable? Who is strong enough to challenge your position at a later date?

- Are there non-traditional distributors whose work encroaches into your product lines? Why would the customer think of them over you and your organization? Price? Delivery? Better information on line? Convenience?

- Does your customer have a plant or companywide specification for new products purchased? Do you know who creates the specification? Are you and your products on the list?

- If your customer uses other suppliers, what specific non-product points do they place a value on with the supplier? This one is tough. Sometimes you have to separate yourself from emotions to be objective on "competitive strengths."

- Are there people at the account who still need to be "won over"? Specifically who are they?

- Ask multiple people at the account this question: What is the greatest value we provide as a supplier? Are the answers consistent? It is not uncommon for different groups within the same account to place a higher value on different areas of your service, support and product offerings.

Part 3

What do you know about your account?

Are we really Selling Solutions?

Everybody claims to be a Solution Seller these days. In the world of selling, it's the place where the cool kids are supposed to be hanging out. To illustrate, a quick "Google" of the term "Solution Selling" turns up something like 246 Million entries. As a group, we are talking the talk, but a deeper dive into the topic make me wonder.

Even the top salespeople in our industry confuse product expertise with providing a customer-centric solution. Is there value in helping your customer select just the right product for their application? Absolutely. Does your troubleshooting assistance provide something important to your customer? No doubt about it. But solution selling extends well beyond this type of product-centric customer support. If the only solution you provide comes via the ability to answer customer questions about products. I suspect you are vulnerable to future competitive threats. Here is why.

We are moving into the next generation of internet and mobile driven apps at breakneck speed. For instance, I recently became aware of a new batch of apps which are comprehensive in the adroit manner they direct a novice customer through the selection of very technical products. Reports of manufacturers and mega-catalog distributors creatively applying cell phone pictures to the problem of identifying obscure parts are increasing exponentially. Companies with internet-based monitoring of "programmable devices" are upping the ante on product-based troubleshooting. Frankly, I see some of these as being game changers in the world of product application expertise for sale.

In days of old, the knowledge-based distributor's "stock in trade" was product expertise. Complex products with lots of nuances demanded and received higher margins than simple products. Very early on, the salesperson acted as a "human search engine" turning the customer's vague request for product information into an assortment of product data sheets. Later, the salesperson translated customer start-up or troubleshooting questions into highlighted pages from the user's manual. Things have changed. The value for this type of service is declining. Where is the real value to be provided?

Here's where we get to the whole solution selling thing. True solution selling calls for an ability to recognize issues and proposing solutions; often before the customer even realizes a problem exists. While products play a role in creating the solution, the real meat of the sale revolves around what you know about the customer. Sadly, we find salespeople lack an understanding of even the simplest aspects of the customer's world. More complex issues are totally ignored.

This brings us back to the original question. What do we really know about the customer?

What do We Really Know about the Customer?
In order to have a meaningful strategic plan for our accounts, we must take a personal and organizational inventory of what we know now and what we have to quickly learn for the future.

Unless your plan revolves around becoming the biggest and best low-price discount parts depot, failure to position ourselves a real life solution providers means slow but certain decline. Further, it could be argued that in some instances, understanding the customer points to needs outside of our expertise. We might even come to the realization that providing solutions to some customers is a poor use of our resources. Stated another way, some customers place a high value on solutions you are either not capable of providing or not willing to execute. Throwing your best efforts at these folks is akin to putting time and money down the proverbial rat hole.

Here are a few items I believe central to building the knowledge needed to create solutions:

How does the customer really make money?
The answer to this question is not always as evident as one might think. For instance, it is not uncommon for some industries to pass their products along at cost in order to sell repair parts over the life of the equipment. Other organizations make strategic decisions to sell certain products at a loss in order to hold their market position open until new technology or new products can be launched. Understanding the difference is of prime importance to building for your mutual future, or in creating your strategic plan for the customer.

Going back to the example of the industry selling products with an eye for lucrative repair parts orders, compare two viable solutions. Solution one allows for quick and easy repair with parts commonly available from suppliers other than the manufacturer. Alternatively, a second solution provides customized part numbers which must be sourced from your customer. Which would have the greatest appeal?

What are the customer's competitive threats?
To help your customer build their business, understand their competitive situation. Is margin under attack from off-shore manufacturers? Is the company struggling to meet new trends in the industry? Are government regulations pushing some of their core products into obsolescence?

Companies concerned about margin erosion are less likely to favor higher end components in their product, but very willing to adopt innovative processes which drive out costs associated with raw materials, production, utilities and other processes. Your new high end gizmo might make their machine last years longer, but they probably won't be interested.

Is your customer part of a larger organization?
Why is this important? Specifications and buying decisions are often driven from headquarters. Investments are tied to the financial performance of the larger parent company. As solutions are presented, it is wise to understand the longer term direction of the larger organization.

If this book detailed the dilemmas faced by every salesperson whose "big account" was gobbled up by a multi-national organization, it would look more like the 28 book encyclopedia I sold back in college. If you happen to be reading this and one of your major commission makers just changed owners, time to reset your strategy; regardless of how many times the customer says, "nothing will change."

How does your customer's sales process work and can you somehow improve it?
Somehow sellers skip over what could be their single best ally at their accounts. Not only can you build immediate comradery with brothers in the selling profession, your customer's salespeople have a front-row view of customer needs. Is something missing from their product which could be developed by your company? Do they fully understand the technologies of new product advancements?

For many smaller companies, conversations with their customer's sales team is equivalent to research and development. Documented cases over the past several decades tell us, the product development for many companies follows closely behind customer requests to the sales and marketing guys in the field.

How might the customer improve their process to decrease expenses, improve output or sell more product?
Many times the solutions you provide literally pay for themselves. If your solution significantly reduces raw material or energy costs, the sale is nearly automatic. If the production process has a bottleneck and you can inexpensively eliminate the issue, you've provided a solution.

Later we'll talk about understanding the monetary value of our solutions, but for now let's say, most solutions become real when they impact the customer in a monetary way. Unless you happen to deal exclusively with the government or not-for-profits, the solution seller's mission in life is to generate more money for customers.

Does the customer have seasons where only a portion of their resources are used?
Seasonal ups and downs drive buying behavior. Understanding the best time to make changes in the process improves your selling efficiency. Further, working to smooth out some of the seasonal swings can increase your chances of providing a viable solution.

Does your customer have issues finding the right people or getting those people trained?
Demographic experts tell us something like 10,000 baby boomers are retiring every day. As this group turns in their job for a spot on the beach, highly trained machine operators, technicians, engineers and others are leaving their employers with critical vacancies. Many companies have discovered a major gap in their ability to recruit and train new hires. Understanding your customer's needs provides an opportunity to fine tune your solutions.

As an extended side note for sales managers reading this book. You may have discovered the same thing happening to your sales team. Perhaps you have seen some of your best seller hand over the keys to their company car and head off to the golf course. If that's the case, I hope this book will serve as a guideline for developing new talent.

What is the burdened cost of labor at your customer?
If you happen to provide solutions which are labor saving, comprehending the cost of the labor saved is critical. Strangely, we hear of automation solution providers touting their ability to replace workers without one iota for knowledge on the cost of the workers replaced by their application. It's not purely about the worker's wage. Health insurance, worker's compensation costs and other factors sometimes double the compensation sent home with the worker; hence the need to understand burdened costs.

As an interesting side note, one leading manufacturer of collaborative robots has built their company's distributor policy around the financial benefits of applying their robots in place of existing workers. Training their sales team and channel partners on plugging in labor costs, the company has learned to predict the opportunity of success on burdened labor rates at customers.

Are unions, skilled trade groups or others part of the customer's environment?
What is the overall relationship with the groups? Do these create special needs? Sometimes union contracts impact the types of solutions available to the customer. For instance, one major white goods manufacturer

signed a union agreement which limited the number of robots which could be installed into their production line. While automation was important to the company's operation, it couldn't come in the form of a robot. Similar issues tied to types of solutions and workflow within the organization abound. Without at least a cursory understanding, a seller could invest significant effort into solutions which cannot be purchased.

What are the raw materials used by the customer?
Do you have an accurate estimate of the cost of the raw materials? If you plan on developing solutions which impact waste, rejects or other material related issues, it pays to understand their cost and sources for the materials. If any of the raw materials are in short supply, solutions might eventually target finding or changing the stuff that goes into the customer's operation.

Does it cost a lot of money to store the materials?
Many distributors provide solutions impacting the storing and handling of the materials sold to the customer. For some suppliers, solutions include gas cylinders, storage tanks, metering equipment and other items tied to the real product sold. Further, it pays to understand whether shrinkage an issue at the customer. Equipment which is lost, damaged in storage or stolen creates a whole new group of solutions to discuss with the customer.

Are there governmental or other regulations that impact the customer's business?
Governmental regulations can impact businesses faster than changing market conditions. No one has experienced this more than companies who manufacturer heating and cooling equipment. Government mandates tied to use of fluorocarbons (tied to climate change) create havoc on product lifecycle plans and obsolescence. Similarly, OSHA regulations have created a whole new industry around machine-guarding and safety interlocks in the electric, fluid power and automation fields. Possessing at least a rudimentary understanding of how these regulations impact your customer's business paves the way for better solutions from your organization.

Is there more? You bet there is.
Understand, this is not an all-encompassing list. Your list will vary based on the type of customer, your own industry and other variables, but you do need to look at each of these as strategic to your own customer's future. Aligning your strategic plan to customer strategy is important to building a plan.

As we look forward...
By now you may have come to the realization a lot of effort goes into building a strategic plan for your accounts. We are mostly done looking at the current situation at the account. With all this work, the importance of figuring out how the account might mesh with your selling time and efforts should weigh heavily on the mind. In the next portion of this book we will look into how we begin setting up some priorities in our attack.

Points to ponder:

- End User administrative costs: If you do business in the MRO world, you should understand this point: a study in 2000 indicated it cost the average large end user $115 to create and execute a purchase order. Do you know what it costs your customer to handle a purchase order?

- OEM issues: Original Equipment Manufacturers (OEMs) often struggle with the logistics to get products into their facility in an organized manner. Getting a shipment for everything needed to complete a machine except for one critical part costs them mega bucks and upsets their operation. Does your company offer services that package all of the parts required to complete a job on time? Is this important to your customer?

- Technology issues: Many companies are struggling to absorb all of the technology available to them. Does your customer have a "wish list" of technology improvements they would like to implement? How might these impact the customer? Are there areas where you could help them gain greater competence?

- People issues: In spite of what you hear on the nightly news, many of our customers are finding it difficult to find the right people to fill technically skilled positions. Can you help them locate the right people? Are there training issues you can help them overcome?

- Production/Job bottlenecks: Does your customer have production or process bottlenecks? What are the implications of fixing them?

- Factory uptime/downtime: Manufacturers around the world are struggling to keep their plants at full capacity. Often, the loss of just a few hours a week to unscheduled downtime creates financial havoc. The need for unplanned overtime drives up labor costs and damages employee morale. Missed customer shipment dates puts a damper on market expansion. Do you know your customer's situation? Can you create solutions which lessen the impact of these issues?

Part 4
Prioritization of Accounts

Just to refresh on the process of building a strategic plan for our accounts: First we talked about knowing where we stand with the account, things like our strengths, whether the customer sees us as a pipsqueak specialty vendor, one of the top suppliers or as their critically important partner in business. Later we covered what you need to know about the account. By now I know many of you are thinking, "I just don't have enough hours in the day to go through this exercise with everyone on my customer list." That is precisely the point we want to address. You don't have enough time.

American Founding Father, Thomas Jefferson said, "All men are created equal." As smart as he was, Jefferson wasn't a top flight salesperson (as a matter of fact he died broke). Smart sellers learn early on, all accounts are *not* created equal. Some will never contribute much to either your book of business or commission check. Figuratively speaking, "blowing up" a high-octane customer puts more to your bottom line than a tiny account. Sales professionals owe it to their families, employers and even themselves to focus efforts on accounts with the ability to add maximum return. Doubling the size of a $20,000/year customer doesn't add near the results of a modest 10 percent growth at a $1M a year account.

We must target to be effective. The question is where to start.

Salespeople have more accounts than time.
Looking over the results of hundreds of distributor sellers indicates to me the power generally lies with the top 15-20 accounts. If we focus our research and strategic thinking on the big guys, we maximize the use of our time.

Not only does focusing efforts on the top of our customer printout help us build business, the effort strengthens our existing relationships. It both an offensive (as in sale growth) and a defensive (as in fending off competitors) play.

Further, I worry we don't have time to spend with many more than 20 accounts anyway. Here is an excerpt from an article I wrote a couple of years ago:

"A stroll through the account assignments of dozens of electrical wholesalers reveals sales guys with 100, 150 or even more accounts to their name. I believe this is a sham.

First let's look at the math.

Number of selling days		160
Calls per day		4
Total number of calls available per year		640
Calls to top 10 accounts	Let's assume the following: • We have multiple contacts • Ongoing business requires 1 call of some kind per week	500
Calls to next 10 accounts	Let's assume the following: • Ongoing business and development of new opportunities requires 1 call per month	120
Total calls remaining		20

Based on experience, after subtracting vacation, holidays, training, office and meetings days, the average seller has around 160 days of selling time per year. If we credit salespeople with 4 real calls per day, this equates to something like 640 calls per year. If we assume a few of the top 10 accounts require a call every week, the salesperson is left with just 140 calls for the rest of the list. I suspect the next 10 on their list require at least one call every month, this leaves us with a whopping 20 calls left for the year."

Now back to "targeting" our planning efforts. I sincerely doubt if extra calls will be required to gather much of the information we have talked about. However, organizing and optimizing around the information does take time and if we really buy into this strategy, we do have 20 calls to invest in the process.

Think about storing account information.
Starting something like this requires a schedule, a strategy and a plan. Why not start with your top five accounts? Hopefully, you know them best. Much of the information may already be floating somewhere in the deep recesses of your brain. Thinking about what you know and, more importantly, what you don't know will open your mind to the topic. But, we do recommend you create a space for storing the information either in writing or electronically. With a little modification, most reputable CRM Systems might become your repository of information.

Why store the information? First, in today's environment, most distributors operate in a team selling fashion. Specialists, Customer Service and Inside Sales groups from your own company regularly touch the customer; quite possibly it's the case with supply partners and other allies. Periodically reviewing information with others provides valuable insights. More importantly, developing a document enables you to start/continue refining your strategic account plan. Many of our long-term plans for positioning require ongoing inventory of our current situation.

I encourage you to create a list that looks like this:

Account: Frank's Widget Warriors (FWW)	
Our Situation	We sell FWW all of their flex tubing, most of their automation needs and some of the gasses used in their process. We are viewed as an important supplier in our category but certainly do not dominate the whole of their available business.
Competitors	• 7Dee Distributing sells more of the process gas than we do. They are viewed as expert and provide low prices when contracts can tie up the business for a long time. • MMark,Inc. provides a portion of their automation needs. Most of these were specified into the plant by their parent company.

	• W&G Distribution sells some of the fittings used with our tubing. They rarely call on FWW. We have crossed over their parts and are ready for the next bidding cycle. • Haven't had time to research other suppliers

What do we know	• The biggest source of their revenue comes sale of complete systems
	• FWW is considering moving spare parts to more of a profit center
	    ○ We are currently looking for metrics and figures.
	• They have rejects – don't know numbers?
	• Burdened Labor on Shop floor - $38.00
	• Burdened cost of Engineering - ???
	• Frank's Widget Warriors' sales team need assistance explaining some technical issues to their customers
	    ○ Working to understand how we can help
	• The energy cost to build full sized widgets is going up rapidly.

Let me sidetrack the conversation for just a moment

I know what a lot of you are thinking. I am too busy. My boss is already asking for reports, projections and a bunch of other stuff. Why should I slow my progress with a bunch of self-induced paperwork? The answer can be derived from two completely different schools of thought.

First, the team sell approach must be considered. The days of the Lone Ranger sales guy fighting for truth, justice and a bigger commission check are over. Nearly every sales group in the country has multiple individuals communicating with customer contacts. Each interaction of the group offers yet another opportunity to gather an important piece of information. All too often this information is wasted. Not because the other team members talking on the phone, answering a customer question or servicing the customer aren't paying attention, but rather because the information wasn't recognized as being critically important to driving the effort forward. To illustrate how important this team play can be, I have dozens of examples of delivery drivers reporting back important competitive information, but only after they were coached on what to look for in the customer's receiving area.

Sharing information helps everyone on the team provide better service. Further, from a selfish standpoint, information in the right hands allows others to understand customer changes in policy and shifts in buying direction. For instance, if a customer service person connected to your account receives a request for a product normally bought from a competitor, they will recognize the significance of the event. A phone call from an engineer who typically favors a competitor might send up a green flag which could be turned into a major breakthrough.

Secondly, and perhaps even more importantly, creating a hard copy of information about the account provides for a new level of objectivity in sales strategy. After more than four decades in the selling business, I have observed: salespeople tend to glamorize their successes and gloss over the time they lost the big order. Could it be the human condition? Am I getting all pop psychologist on you? It happened to me back in my territory days. Many of the top sellers I have interviewed claim the same phenomenon. Experts (armed with real research data) detail two points. One, the best sellers are optimistic; they always imagine getting the sale. And two, those who create written goals achieve more than their counterparts who fail to commit the information to hard (written or entered in a computer) form.

Upon each review on the information gathered for your top accounts, some new piece of information will come to mind. Because the information is "journaled" gaps in information will become more evident. By periodically reviewing previously collected customer information, sellers can measure progress.

Finally, then I will quit whipping this horse along, listing information acts as a hedge against poor memory. Think for just a moment, with fifty or more accounts, a dozen or so contacts at each account, thousands of products in play and a cadre of supply partners pulling at a seller's coattails it is darned easy to occasionally drop a ball. Professionals hedge against this by creating a repository of information for their accounts.

Now, back to our prioritization of accounts discussion.
Experience shows most salespeople don't really prioritize their accounts. A good many sellers work in a reactive mode where they endear themselves to customers by providing quick reaction to ongoing issues. I won't argue the validity of this approach. A few sellers are actually very successful using this set up. However, there are issues. For one, a new guy using this approach spends lots of time waiting to be called out to serve the customer. Further, the new product/technology sales cycle is extremely long and breaking into new accounts only happens when the sun, moon and stars are in complete alignment.

We will take a more detailed look at sizing up customers in a later chapter, but for now let's think about selling in the abstract. We will start with a premise. People buy from those they know and trust. Who knows and, hopefully, trusts you? Most agree, the answer is your top customers. Perhaps this explains the phenomenon pronounced by so many selling experts - it is five times easier to sell more to existing accounts than to sell to new accounts.

When we talk to new sellers, they lay out plans to drive business across the board. They speak in glowing terms of doubling the business at a number of low performing accounts. But the math doesn't work out. Doubling a $10,000 account barely moves the commission dollar dial. Even doubling three or four smaller accounts lacks the same impact as increasing a half million dollar account by a measly 10 percent.

Restating the point, I recommend focusing your attention on your top few accounts. It's my hypothesis you believe you have fully penetrated a couple of these accounts. You get lots of business, everyone there likes you and walking down the customer's hallway is old home week. Does it make sense to build a strategic plan for these accounts? Most believe it does and here's why.

Building a strategic plan is a good defensive measure.
Count on one fact, there are sellers out there salivating over the dollars you generate. Your business falls right in the crosshairs of their growth plans. The smart ones attack the fringes; picking up orders for some of your marginal products. I call these guys ankle biters; constantly nipping

at the few products in your portfolio which lack the technological charm or low price points of something in their catalog or line card. Further, their strategy allows them to position for that fateful day when your own organization is short on stock, screws up an order or drops the ball on some hot project (it happens).

Building a strategic plan allows you to better understand the all of the account dynamics. You take the time to identify your best allies and those who may not appreciate your work. You examine your relationship with the customer's top brass. Examine the customer's future direction and you become more aware of the potential changes far ahead of the competition. Let's go back in time and review the story of one such meeting.

Illustrating the importance of understanding customer direction.
Some of this will sound strange, but back in 1998 there were a great many people predicting major collapses in global infrastructure based on the change of the century. The three or four years leading up the December 31, 1999 overflowed with Y2K prognostications. Experts zigzagged across the country predicting everything from power grid failure to massive breakdown of the banking system. Even mainstream folks horded canned foods; just in case. Building an account based strategic plan brought me in contact with the plant manager of a meat canning facility.

The plant manage shared a plan to shift and maximize product output until December of 1999 and then quickly change to something else once the mad rush to stock "survivalist shelves" was done. He went on to say, anything they purchased would be judged based on its ability to be quickly repurposed.

All of this was news to the salesperson calling on the account. Later we learned many of the plant operations people (who were the seller's day to day contacts) had yet to be briefed. One can only wonder what might have happened if we hadn't carried out the exercise. Did it provide a strategic advantage at the canning factory? Looking back, I believe it did.

Let's go on the offense.
Skipping over the couple of accounts that you virtually "own", let's look at the rest of your top 10 accounts. It is possible to launch five or ten fairly

comprehensive strategic plans over a 45-60 day period. Sitting with your team, you can quickly identify areas were examination is needed. You will have multiple call opportunities to verify information and ask several existing contacts their opinion on your service, competitors and even the customer's own challenges in the market.

What's really cool about working a strategic plan? Many of the customer contacts privy to the information you need are on your normal call schedule. There is no need to make separate appointments, do lots of extra running around or any of the other time wasters associated with chasing down a new account. Looking backward, you could have asked them many of these questions months or even years ago. You just didn't think of it. Now you have a plan.

Looking forward...
As we move forward, we will focus our attention toward growing our relationship and building a strong mutually beneficial business with each of these important customers. Jumping back onto my "write down your plan" soapbox, allow me to assume you are putting what you know into some kind of journal or CRM System. Armed with what we know about each of our strategic accounts, let's journey forward and invest time in the value we bring to the customer. We are not leaving customer knowledge behind. Instead, the next step in the strategic plan is understanding how our work brings value to the customer. Allow me to warn you, value is not generic. The value we provide to customers is specific, very specific

Point to Ponder:

- Frank's Soapbox – You are probably sick of this but: How will you store what you know at each account? This concept worked back in the dark ages when paper was the only median for keeping lists, so I suspect there are tons of creative sales guys armed with iPads, tablet computers and handy apps for keeping track of what they know. The important point is keep track of the right information. Who is the customer? Where do we sit with the customer, including competition and product/service specifications? And what do we really know about the customer? Incidentally, the last one will be long and, hopefully, ever expanding.

- If you happen to "own" an account or two, answer the following. When was the last time you analyzed sales by product line? Are there products that naturally "go with" what you sell that are not purchased from you? Have you taken time to visit their internal storeroom or parts crib? Have you asked someone on the financial side of the business their view of your products and service?

- Can I do more than ten accounts: You've got an account or two that fall outside of your top 10 that you feel could drive some real dollars to your sales totals, you have a foot in the door and things are progressing nicely, why not develop a strategic plan for them as well? I worry about the time factor of developing too many strategic plans at once. But, if you insist. Here's a suggestion. Select one of your top accounts that you feel doesn't necessary deserve special treatment; perhaps it is becoming price driven or is in an industry which is in decline. Then make a carefully weighed decision to replace it with the up and comer.

Part Five
What value do you bring to the customer?

Several months ago, I had the opportunity to "ride along" with a guy my client described as "one of our promising new sales guys." I wanted to just get a snapshot of the quality and quantity of this guy's work, so I didn't do much to brief him on our objectives for the day. Instead, I emailed, "I just want to ride along and observe a typical work day." A few days later, he texted coordinates of a greasy spoon diner where we would slosh down a cup of coffee and brace ourselves for the day.

After a handshake and a few social niceties, we dove into the day ahead. I was pleased. He had real live appointments at three accounts and plans to drop by another couple if time allowed. Demos and literature were well thought out and carefully stored in the back seat of his meticulously cleaned company car. He had invested in timely topics to explore with the various people scheduled to see us. I could easily see why this guy impressed the boss.

The "same ole" value story...
During our 30 minute drive to the first appointment, we talked about his company; locations, people, size, products on their line card and lots of sundry details. These folks were on the move. About midway into our drive, I asked, "What kind of value do you deliver to the customer?" The answer was both typical and scary; something to the effect of, "We have the best service in the whole area." In spite of a couple of unfocused pushes, the best I could get was "better outside sales", "better customer service" and a "willingness to listen."

This is an all too common response. And it's epidemic in our industry. For knowledge-based distributors it could be a fatal flaw.

What are some real values?

How should have the sales guy have responded? A detailed list of services provided to customers would have been a nice start. Here are a dozen examples:

1. Policy of stocking emergency inventory to assist customers during emergency and downtime situations.

2. Afterhours access to inventory and staff in emergency situations.

3. Ongoing customer training sessions including one-on-one training for new engineers, maintenance personnel and others.

4. Ability to handle blanket orders and provide summary billing which drives down the customer's administrative costs.

5. Inventory services to assist customers with managing consumable parts.

6. Willingness to join customer in tri-lateral negotiations (Special Pricing Agreements) to improve costs on high volume purchases.

7. Salespeople with technical backgrounds capable of assisting in the selection of the best product for the customer's application.

8. Highly trained Product Specialists who assist with product concepts and layouts.

9. Troubleshooting assistance with technical products.

10. In-house value add group with capabilities to provide complete sub-assemblies ready for installation.

11. Engineers and Specialists who work with customers to "value engineer" existing designs in search new technology and/or products with better fit with the goal of driving down unit costs.

12. Willingness to source hard to find parts which drive up administrative costs at the customer.

Is this a complete list? I doubt it. Most distributors we work with can come up with 20-50 more things they do to provide value to their customers. The point is you have something to sell above and beyond the products shipping from your warehouse. A good strategic plan pulls selected services from the list. Why? Because not all of your services match up with every customer, but you need to have a very solid grip on what's available before you can proceed with your plan.

Defining value

Way back in the 1970s, Feature/Benefit selling was the rage. You detailed your product one feature at a time; matching corresponding customer benefits to each feature. Average performers simply reiterated the complete feature/benefit set for every customer presentation. It sounded like the drone of a skipping record.

Somewhere around 1984 value-added selling entered the sales lexicon. Using today's internet slang, the idea quickly went viral. Since the turn of the last century, finding a sales organization that doesn't expound some version of value-add mentality is darned hard. With all this value talk, one would imagine an understanding of value would be mandatory. Yet, most salespeople have a difficult time defining the term.

What's in the standard distributor sales presentation?

Just for fun, we will take a look at points from the standard distributor sales presentation; most of which create zero customer value. The history of the company is mighty interesting but it creates no value. The mission and vision statement sound flowery, but value? I don't think so. The shiny new building called corporate headquarters shows the distributor might be successful, but it doesn't do a darn thing for customers. Taking the risk of sounding calloused and mean, your ESOP ownership is mostly cool for the folks working for your company but isn't a value a customer can "hang their hat on."

What is real customer value?

Value improves the customer's lot. It has everything to do with the customer and nothing to do with you, your company or even your industry. Since most of the readers come from the ranks of knowledge-based distribution, allow me to say this. Many customers start off questioning the value of distribution. Constantly bombarded with messages to avoid the middleman and save, these folks wonder if they could do better by simply striking up a deal with the manufacturer directly. We distributors only exist because of the value we provide to our customers. Simply stated: Distributors create value which cannot be provided by the manufacturer directly, by some parts warehouse in China shipping thousands of boxes into the area or even by the fanciest of internet websites. What's more, the value we provide today is completely different than the value of 20 years past or 10 years into the future.

Value equates to something we do to make the customer more efficient, productive or profitable. There are thousands of things you can do to achieve the result but most of them break down into seven categories.

1) Eliminate some of the labor provided by those inside the organization.

2) Eliminate the labor of outside organizations sometimes hired by the customer.

3) Increase the amount of sellable product or service produced.

4) Reduce the amount of product wasted due to process issues.

5) Reduce expenses spent on raw materials, utilities, insurance or other materials.

6) Improve the value of products sold via market position or quality.

7) Drive cultural issues like improved worker safety, workplace environment or "social responsibility" goals. (This one is hard to identify and quantify unless you have a solid customer relationship.)

Looking at the example of a product which increases a factory's uptime, we could impact each of the following: The need for unplanned overtime required to make up for lost productions, the amount of product produced, and in some cases, product waste created (because it sat in a state of near completion and somehow was spoiled).

Value is customer specific.
Not every product we sell or service we provide impacts customers universally. Going to a ridiculous extreme, the auto license plates used in Iowa are made by inmates of the Department of Corrections. My

unsubstantiated guess is Prison Industries is not all that concerned with eliminating labor costs. However, they may be very interested in buying parts which lack sharp edges which undoubtedly improves worker safety.

While this little blurb on the nuances of license plates is goofy, it drives home a point. Value is seen differently by every customer. An astute salesperson gathers information about their customer and aligns the products and services in their catalog to match specific customer needs. These morph into their value to that customer. While similar customers experience similar needs, I would not suggest assuming value can be dished out carte blanc. The value idea works best (perhaps only) when applied to exactly one customer at a time.

Additionally, care must be taken to closely match values with the right person at the account. For instance, in example five (5) above we noted the distributor has the ability to assist the customer in managing consumables. No doubt, the customer contact charged with the task of inventory may see this service as a potential threat to job security. At the same time and just down the hall, a facilities manager concerned with driving performance may see this as a valuable key to reassigning the inventory guy to something more productive.

Thinking more deeply; in most instances, it pays to bring your values to the customer in an order which is well thought out. Some values are expensive to provide. Other values may be less defined than an incumbent competitor. This dovetails back to the power of a strategic plan for each major account.

These value questions demand answers.
Where might you easily demonstrate your ability to provide value? Once that value has been demonstrated, how can you expand into other areas of increasing importance? Are there competitors which could easily be displaced and their business rolled into your cart?

It's never enough to just provide value. Get feedback from your customers. Customer emails detailing how you helped solve a problem open other doors to sales. Ask the customer if they will send an email you can share with a supplier or your boss. Even if the customer hesitates to send you some documentation, create your own log of actions, values provided and other milestones at the account.

Never try to introduce multiple values at the same time. While they do make for a great capabilities presentation, too many choices confuse the customer. Instead, work to understand the customer's own priorities. Gather the kind of data we spoke about earlier in Part 3. Ask additional questions and introduce your value; one step at a time.

A final couple of thoughts...
Going back for a moment to the concept of matching value to the contact at the account. Often, sellers will discover they lack the proper audience for laying out some of their biggest value creation ideas. Sellers who limit themselves to just calling on the purchasing department probably aren't reading this book. However, the world is full of sellers who focus so heavily on technical, maintenance or operational people, they totally miss the opportunity to speak to the group who can most easily open the door for financial success. In the next section, we will talk about who to know at these strategic accounts.

Points to Ponder:

- Let's play a little game. I call it the good, the bad and the ugly. Thinking back to your last customer presentation. You know, the one with a half dozen customers in the room and you standing at the front playing PowerPoint. What portions of your presentation were good because they dealt directly with how you might impact one of the seven (7) value drivers we laid out above? What bits of badness did you ladle into your presentation (things like company history, your many locations or your growth curve)? What was so boringly ugly most of the customers decided to check email on their cell phones? Ugly typically comes in flowery mission statements, details of products the customer doesn't use or anything else that's specifically impacting the customer group.

- Think about a time you provided some product or ancillary service for one of your top 5 accounts. Which of the seven value drivers were affected? Do you have an idea as to the monetary impact?

- Many distributors tout the value of their "highly trained" inside sales or customer service representatives. Take just a moment to list a few specific instances where your team created value for one of your top 5 accounts. Which of the value drivers did they touch against?

- Soul searching required. Have you bloviated on some special service in the past and later discovered the customer wasn't all that impressed? Did your "special service" lack the "special sauce" required to make a difference in any of the seven value drivers mentioned?

Part 6
Sometimes, it's not what you know, but who you know

You've heard the saying, "Sometimes, it's not what you know, but who you know that counts." Perhaps, you've been on the wrong end of this old axiom. You did your homework, researched products, built a killer presentation and followed up with amazing vigor; only to lose an opportunity to someone who had a relationship with the customer's top brass. These things happen and seemingly there is really nothing you can do about it. As salespeople we can either shrug our shoulders and go on about our day, or do something about the situation.

Most salespeople focus on the technical users of their products. For automation sellers, it's the engineering department. Industrial supply salespeople hit on maintenance. Janitorial and paper product distributor sales folks go to the head of facilities. I could elaborate on the list to nauseating length, but the point is most frontline sellers focus on a narrow group of contacts at their customer. Strategically, this is a mistake.

Let's fast forward, your efforts at an account are successful. Your company starts landing some really meaningful orders. You find yourself harvesting big dollars from the account. All of your contacts appreciate the service you provide. Somebody, somewhere is writing (or at least signing) significantly large checks to your organization. Does it seem strange you don't know them? But then, something happens.

The C-Level end around defined.
A new supplier does an end around and goes straight to the money guys. By-passing all the product knowledge, expert services and other goodies

you provide, they deliver a compelling pitch on how they can save your customer money. Suddenly, you're on the defensive.

Don't believe this can happen? Let me reference you to Chapter 5 of <u>The Challenger Sale</u>, where authors Dixon and Adamson go step by step through the selling model W.W. Grainger unleashed on the unsuspecting industrial sector. Basically, Grainger did an end around and created a new model for MRO purchasing. In many instances it worked. The model focused on the administrative cost of MRO purchases. Grainger's successes sent a legion of high quality, service focused incumbent salespeople scurrying to save their hard earned business. The strategy spread from the industrial sector onward to electrical, fluid power, mechanical and other lines of wholesale trade.

From a distance, the whole phenomenon seemed predictable. Distributors doing hundreds of thousands with large manufacturing facilities were caught asleep at the wheel. Across North America, distributor managers came to the sad realization, the highest level contacts nurtured at one of their heavy weight accounts was the storeroom clerk, purchasing agent and maintenance supervisor. When the VP of Operations demanded a switch in buying habits, their best buddy acquiesced without a peep.

The point of this? It is impossible to have a solid strategic plan at your account without covering the financial side of the customer.

Who gets compensated on the Customer's Bottom Line?

Every customer on your list has a person who is compensated by bottom line profitability. It could be the profitability of the company, a single plant, a product category or (as is sometimes the case) a single production line; but somewhere a person exists with responsibility for the bottom line. For the sake of our argument, let's call this group of people Top Management. Bordering somewhere between stupidity and disaster in the making, not establishing a relationship with the upper level folks is a major-league mistake.

Most salespeople lack the training necessary to work with Top Management. Even more are lulled into inactivity because they accept one (or more) of the following legends as truth.

Calling on Top Management will alienate existing contacts. Ranking number one on the top guy call reluctance list, this story almost holds water. Sellers of technical products especially convince themselves and their colleagues of the validity of this statement. That gruff guy heading up the engineering department could easily take offense with my efforts to "go over his head".

Never mind the point of building a relationship with the Top Guy has nothing to do with technology plans or actual buying decisions, a short interview would lead to retaliation or business being directed to others.

The people I work with are the ultimate decision makers. Ask any purchasing guy on the planet if they are the ultimate decision maker and 99.9 percent will answer to the affirmative. Experience shows, all but the newest members of the selling world know the real decisions are made elsewhere else within the customer's facility. One of the first serious tools added to every new salesperson's toolbox is a plan for smoothly steering around the purchasing department. Yet, once they arrive in the technical group, they get a new impression, these folks are the end of the decision making process.

To test the theory, reflect back on projects put on hold because they lacked funding. How many times has one of your "ultimate decision makers" remarked about new equipment being dropped in from another plant or sister division? In calls with hundreds of salespeople working territories just like yours, I have encountered dozens of instances where engineering managers, maintenance managers, office managers and others with authority commenting on surprise direction from somebody, somewhere in management. Could it be they really aren't the decision maker?

Top Management guys don't want to be bothered. This one is partially true. Top Management guys don't want to waste time. A sales guy hammering Top Management with product minutia, gibberish about your company's commitment to quality or the latest "double-diphthong hydrister" added to your vendor's technology will soon be put onto the ignore list. These guys don't care about your product or your wonderful service, they care about results. Results are measured in dollars and cents; the kind of values discussed earlier matter.

A seller can either be seen as a bother, and ignored, or seen as a guy who understands a portion of the customer's business and assists in creating additional value. Top Managers place a high regard on individuals capable of creating value. Stories of great salespeople migrating to top positions within one of their important customers bolsters the argument. Salespeople who add value and build relationships with Top Management grow their power, income and status.

Salespeople don't have the background to talk to Top Management.
When young salespeople talk about management, diversity of background always comes up. Things like economic status, hobbies, country club membership and age are laid out as rock solid reasons for not establishing a selling relationship with Top Management individuals. In many instances, they may have a point.

At the same time, evidence points to example after example of Top Management individuals placing exceeding high value on identifying and connecting with promising "up and comers". Many openly share their desire to mentor those they feel worthy of their time and efforts. Partnering with an individual capable of providing insights from a younger perspective holds a place of importance. However, in the case of sellers, they come to the meeting with a natural prejudice based on other encounters which bring little except company propaganda and product spews.

Here is the scoop on Upper Management types.
Regardless of your age and background, best practices in the selling world point to the importance of knowing and understanding the prospective of your customer contact. With this in mind, here are a few things to consider when dealing with this type of customer contact:

- Top Management types are massively busy. You only have a few minutes to impress. Be prepared. Hold initial small talk to a minimum.

- Financial folks really don't understand your product. For the most part, they don't really care for a tutorial. Instead, they want to understand the financial impact of the ideas, solutions and services you bring to their organizations.

- Most of these people complain their technical people don't truly understand all of the financial ramifications of their actions. So if you've been counting on others to share your high end value story, it probably is not working.

- The best will not openly question the decisions of their teams. Never launch a relationship with commentary critical of previous actions.

Thoughts on setting up a meeting with Customer Management.
We need to establish a relationship with management people at important accounts. There are a number of strategies for setting up meetings with this type of person. We won't go into all of them, but here are a couple of my favorites.

Set up an introductory interview. Note interview, as opposed to sales call. In this meeting we quickly introduce ourselves as a supplier of critical goods and services to their organization. Then launch into a few well selected questions on market conditions affecting their company, difficulty finding technically qualified new people, issues impacting their bottom line and their view of the future. That's it. No selling, no elaborate product demos, and no fancy worded mission statement presentations.

Set up customer satisfaction review – In this instance, you essentially thank the management guy for previous business. Let them know you are working to assist in getting the most bang for their buck and ask for feedback on how the whole thing might have worked better. Again, no selling.

It's not a one and done process...
After these first meetings, find an excuse to arrange a similar type of meeting every few months. Short and sweet, with lots of opportunity for the customer's top brass to give you their feedback. If possible, introduce your organizations leadership to the customer's high ranking management. We are going to devote a chapter to using your boss, but

for now think about this: Doesn't it make sense for your manager and your customer's manager to know one another?

Armed with information from our customer's Top Management, we can think more strategically in how we allocate time to our customers. In the next chapter, we are going to revisit the way we think about the opportunities our customers present to our sales plan. Before you move ahead, I strongly suggest you devote a few weeks to "touching" the top guys at your biggest and best accounts. There are a number of exercises listed below to steer you in the process.

Points to Ponder:

- Do you know the names of Top Management at your ten biggest/best accounts? These are people like the owner, VP of Production, Production Manager, VP Operations, Operations Manager, VP of Sales, Manager of Technical Services and maybe Engineering Manager.

- What do you believe is the biggest obstacle for establishing a relationship with your Top Management contact? Are the obstacles tied to your own knowledge of the customer organization? Do you understand the economics of their business? Could they produce more if downtime was eliminate and if so, how might you impact downtime? Could they save money on raw materials if they used your product? Be sure to arm yourself with some facts...

- List out some business oriented questions you would like to explore with the Top Management individual. To get you started here are some sample questions:

  1. My conversations with people in production indicate you are experiencing bottlenecks with production of the controller assembly? Would a work-around solution help you sell more machines?

  2. Does the rising cost of electrical usage impact your ability to meet profit goals? Are you exploring options for energy conservation?

  3. How do you see the business climate for your company's products changing over the next five years?

  4. Can you help me understand the financial impact of a remote service call from your engineering team?

  5. Safety regulations seem to be effecting many of our customers, which regulations do you feel might have the greatest impact on your facility?

- Think of places where your products and services have improved another different customer's operation. Can you relate the story and draw contrasts to this customer's operation? What are the similarities and what are the differences? Can you explain the whole thing in non-technical terms?

- Are there past examples where you worked with this account to create an improvement? What was the improvement? Who in the plant is aware of it? Can you describe your work in a non-egotistical way?

- Many salespeople ignore gathering information from the customer's sales and marketing team. Have you met the head of sales? Are their customers asking for modifications or options with which you might be able to assist with? Are there places where you might provide a part of the necessary training required by their sales team?

- Does the owner/VP of Sales/branch manager of your company know any of the management team at one of your top accounts? Readers who work in smaller markets may discover the owner (or some other leader) from your company has a social connection with the leadership at a strategic account. It is not uncommon for those with large social networks to avoid business discussions during their outings. Many consider it rude to talk business while sipping wine at the big symphony gala. Others openly talk business. If your boss is slow to set up a meeting or sketchy in providing details, you will most likely need to go it alone.

Part 7
How to Think About Opportunities

At the mere mention of the word opportunity, most sales guys' nostrils flare, blood pressure spikes and pupils dilate. Perhaps left over from some prehistoric caveman fight or flight gene, they seem to check their cognitive skills at the door and wildly rush ahead. Make no mistake, I like aggressive sellers. But, it's important to take just a moment to fully understand the full story at an account before investing time, effort and company resources.

The full story comes at the crossroads of three very important variables:
- Real dollars/gross margin potential

- Estimated time to achieve business success

- Level of effort involved with getting the business

Dollar/Gross Margin potential is important.
Many experienced salespeople misjudge the dollar/gross margin potential of their accounts for number of good reasons. Often, it's hard to get accurate estimates of the potential in the early stages of account development. This is one of the reasons we believe strategic planning works best with top accounts. The seller's access to information is better. An understanding of the customer's own ability to accurately forecast and project exists. Historical sales figures provide clues to future buying trends.

Very little of this customer-centric data exists with new accounts or those lower on the customer list. Unless something dramatic happens that provides great insight on the customer, and they do occur on rare occasions, I recommend gathering data and better understanding the customer prior to building a full blown strategic plan. You will find a good many of the techniques and ideas presented as part of the strategic planning process useful and I am fully aware some of you will race ahead ignoring this advice. Excuse me if I repeat myself (after all I am getting long in the tooth) but I would prefer you build strategic plans for your biggest accounts first. It is inherently easier to sell more the same people than to find, develop and close new customers.

Returning to our abilities to estimate potential, most salespeople tend to be wrong in a good many of their estimates regarding accounts. This phenomenon occurs by way of training deficiencies. Further, oftentimes the level of thought put in to actually forecasting and thinking of the opportunity lags behind product and application knowledge.

Salespeople of the future must fully develop these currently lacking skills. The ability to accurately forecast order volume grows in business importance. Using the last recession (The Recession per media hype) as an example, the sellers of most small companies not only missed anticipating the massive drop off in new business, but also erred on the upturn as well. Recessions and recoveries have been a part of the economic cycle since the dawn of the industrial age. However, the acceleration of the cycle has increased the need for more reasonable forecasts. We heartedly recommend sales managers work with their teams to develop forecasting skills. Nothing builds muscle like exercise. Similarly, applying thought to potential at a handful of accounts hones a portion of the skillset. This plays well in the team's ability to measure future potential not only in critical/key accounts (where a strategic plan is developed), but in all accounts under their charge.

Beware of Procurement Department data.
A number of methods exist to gather information around real customer potential. As I like "good examples of bad behavior," one of the worst methodologies is via purchasing departments. Industry experience dictates purchasing/procurement groups are trained to overestimate purchase dollars in order to improve their negotiating positions. The concept of volume discounts and a resulting lower unit price is part of their lexicon. A few purchasing types will outright lie, others will lead you on with words like, "We believe 100,000 units is not out of the question"

which translates into "If the sun, the moon and the stars fall into alignment and the good fairy visits us daily to solve productions issues, we might hit 100,000 units in one of our dreams."

Generalizations don't stand the test of close scrutiny. There may be a few honest procurement types at your customer. You may have developed a strong enough level of partnership with a few of your top customers to end the purchasing dance and may actually receive accurate purchasing information. A review of past behavior and the customer's historical willingness to partner provides data for your decision, but I believe it is wise to initially approach the information handed to you on a silver platter with a degree of skepticism.

Benchmarking is a good start.
One of the best ways to check buying potential is via benchmarking (contrast and comparison) against similar accounts with verified data. This might be a customer of similar size in the same industry. Or, the estimates might come through ratios derived from complementary product groupings. For example, the number of printers sold into a legal office might provide a reasonable estimate of printer cartridges used per year. Stretching the concept of ratios forward, a client in the coin operated laundry industry tells me the Government has developed ratios of water used to numbers of dollars generated by the washing machines in laundromats (which is a cash industry where underreporting of income was once rampant). It is not uncommon to see rules of thumb which give an overall better understanding of potential.

Establishing a best estimate on a product by product basis gives you understanding not only of your market share within the customer, but also provides a picture of products the customer is not buying from your organization. For many years, I have suggested our clients use a FOCUS (Fraction of Catalog USed) analysis to contrast product groups sold to the customer against one another using the types of relationships explained above. (For the price of an email to River Heights Consulting, I will provide you with an example and instructions for creating a FOCUS analysis.)

What is the timeline to success?
Let's break away from the money discussion and move on to another important point; the length of time required to reach personal growth goals. While it might feel good to say, someday we are going to turn this account in to a million dollar deal, "someday" does not create much towards establishing a real strategic plan. Typically, salespeople are judged by their ability to produce growth and attain goals in a timely manner. Therefore, establishing a real timeline is important.

Breaking progress at specific accounts into easy to manage and measurable steps is not only strategically important, but prudent tactically as well. In a previous chapter, we talked about the necessity of gathering customer-centric data. This includes information regarding the customer's own business model, plans for growth and operation parameters within the organization. Certainly, one of our measurable milestones might be the completion of subsets of this data. Putting realistic estimates of chronology required to learn about the customer is part of the timeline process. Salespeople will discover some customers are easy to navigate; answers to tough questions are openly provided. Other customers require more time and effort. The period required to accomplish the task is as much dependent on the customer as the seller.

How quickly does the customer change?
Because a portion of the overall strategy at each strategic account is to increase our importance and therefore attract more business, removal and replacement of small competitors is a reasonable timeline goal. To redefine our goal, we might plan for the tactical elimination short line suppliers selling only one or two SKU's to the account. Similarly, the plan could call for the attack and replacement of companies selling products (and no service) via the internet. The strategic plan will include a realistic timeframe for achieving this task. We must ask ourselves, how quickly does the account make vendor changes when prompted with a better alternative? Experience points out, some companies respond quickly and others put off making changes for months. Either way, our plan is impacted.

As a sidebar for those working on replacing small suppliers at their strategic customers. The customer's cost for administering and dealing with small suppliers is quite high; especially in an MRO environment. If you know an approximate cost of managing a purchase order at your customer, this data could be used to justify paying a little more for the same product purchased from you. Obviously, getting paid more should be part of your strategy, too.

Are there process driven timelines?

Another timeline goal might be the insertion of your company in to the internal processes of the customer. These include activities such as inventory and crib management, parts kitting, building sub-assemblies, or anything putting you in a place where you directly mesh with the customer. Instances where your team actually replaces or enhances the customer's staff strengthens your position and moves you closer to your longer term strategic goal. Beating the drum one more time, what is a realistic timeframe for accomplishing this process?

The timeline for engaging your Team comes into play.

Bringing the strength of other member of your own team to the account might also be one of your time-centric milestones. If your company is one of the many using product managers, specialists, or other support people, why not add dates for their introduction and interaction with the customer? Any activity which creates a new connection between your company's management team and the customer's top brass is extremely valuable. Hence, date-based milestones should most definitely include connection of your management team. Stay tuned, we cover how to put your boss to work in a later chapter.

Remember, this information must be managed with timelines and dates. The ultimate goal is something which allows us to say something like, "By December of next year, we will have accomplished steps one, two and three. Step four will happen by March first." Each specific and measurable activity moves us closer to the strategically dominant position at the customer. Understanding how much time it will take to accomplish each task allows a better gage of the opportunity. Further, it will answer the question, will this account provide major growth in six months or a couple of years?

How much effort will be required?

One of the questions salespeople must consider is, how easy or difficult will it be to get this work accomplished? Let's just think about it for a moment. Some accounts require massive hand holding, others require lots of technical resources and still more are slow to adopt change.

Some types of accounts are easier.
An example which springs to mind contrasts OEMs and End User Accounts. Many companies select the OEM sector to maximize early stage revenue without clogging administrative flow of small one piece orders. By focusing efforts early on, they build volume without need for extensive infrastructure. While the sales cycle for OEMs can be years, the strain on resources is lower than other accounts.

The difference in account types is not exclusively centered on the OEM/End User example. Some companies have discovered customer segments which best match their own internal organization. Perhaps it's the type of services offered, the application expertise of the support team or any of a dozen things, but most sellers discover they "mesh" with some types of customers better than others.   It's definitely worth exploring. Ask yourself does our company think about different types of customers and the stress and strain put on our organization in the form of shipping, warehousing, logistical or other requirements? Why have these targets been established? Generally, going outside of the boundaries of your company's sweet spot means extra work.

Business practices impact the timeline.
In addition, some accounts are noted for poor or at least incompatible business behaviors. It might be safe to say, if one of your customers operates in unstable financial conditions (cash flow issues, highly cyclical order flow, credit issues), extra effort might be spent clearing orders through your credit department and/or collecting payment for your efforts.   I am not saying this automatically disqualifies any account from strategic status. Instead, I believe the seller must understand two things. First, selling time is a precious commodity; time must be invested wisely. Secondly, a certain amount of time, effort and expense will be devoted to the account for non-selling activities. Strategic plans carefully weigh the risks versus rewards.

Price driven behavior can be another incompatible business practice. Customers exist who buy exclusively on price; they constantly shop for the lowest unit price on the planet. A few of them even place massive buys which entice sellers from competitors far and wide to play their game. Because many salespeople somehow believe they can use price to "get in the door" then gradually improve profitability over time, the selling world takes the bait and lines up to provide detailed quotations and extra value-add service in hopes of someday making an acceptable margin.

For the point of the discussion, let's assume you aren't working for a bargain basement discount house and you aren't the lowest cost provider in the world. Instead, you provide strong support, value-adds and work to help your customers be more competitive. Based on previous portions of this book, you understand what those are the financial impact to the customer.

Strategically speaking, an account with high potential and a bargain basement mentality may not play a role in your longer term success. Salespeople ultimately work for gross margin dollars. This is true even if your commission is based on top line sales. Touching on the old "lose a little bit on every transaction and make it up on volume" joke, at some point, every company has to produce a profit.

I recommend you approach the price situation carefully. Very few companies post a sign over their door saying, "We buy only on price." It's a complicated issue, price-driven guys will tell you price is number five on their buying criteria. Value-oriented customers sometimes appear price oriented; especially when they fail to understand your value. At some point, you will understand the company's behavior. Since our focus has been on the top five or ten accounts and you probably know them well, use what you know to drive your decision.

What we want to look for are opportunities with a large chance of success and a minimum of effort. These are topics which require deep thought. Most salespeople never take a step back from their customer interaction to answer the question, "Is this really an account capable of taking me to the next level?"

Thinking about the balance of Effort, Time and Potential.
On first glance, the thought of strategically identifying the properties of an account based on these three categories is daunting. However, failure

to recognize their interaction can send a salesperson's efforts whirling down the drain.

The huge potential available at an account might outweigh the lower scores in the time and effort categories. Most sales professionals are charged with an account portfolio. Some possess lower potential but are otherwise easy to convert; these are the legendary "low hanging fruit" of sales. Others offer massive gains but require massive time commitments to convert and still more fall out of your organization's sweet spot.

There is no "one size fits all" approach. Good judgment and careful evaluation are the responsibility of the salesperson. Build a team; bring your company's leadership, other experienced sellers or other trusted advisers into the discussion. Allow one more point: Don't ask the team (especially company leadership) to make a decision for you. Instead, use the team to help you make better decisions by challenging your thought process.

Customer specific research, data, analytics and an unemotional review of past behavior is part of the account evaluation. Far too often, sales planning discussions enter the "data free zone". The best practice for involving others includes a review of the facts. Again, the salesperson should actively encourage others on their team to challenge the facts presented and provide sources for additional information. Remember, some will state subjective opinion as data. When this happens, press for real data to substantiate their opinion.

Remember, skipping this step because it is difficult will not only hamper your progress, it will ultimately impact your success. In the next chapter, we'll hit on the flow of money. Selling by definition involves the customer handing over some of their hard won cash. We all place a value on money, but most sellers fail to think about how it flows within the customer organization.

Points to Ponder:

- Real Dollars/gross margin potential can be derived in a number of ways. How did you arrive at your estimate? Customer information gathered from a number of sources? Comparisons against other companies in the same or similar industries? Some industry rule of thumb? For instance, Electrical Wholesaling Magazine publishes a market planning guide. Based on their guide an Electrical Contractors purchases nearly $50,000 per electrician employed and an industrial manufacturer buys about $600 per employee.

- What is the estimated time associated with obtaining the business? Can this be broken down into various products or groups of products? Which product or technology is most likely to be converted first? Are you going after the easy business first? If you gain this business, what does it do to improve your position for the rest?

- Level of effort involved with getting the business

    1. Does this customer fall into your organization's sweet spot?

    2. Will you need to develop additional programs or services to gain the business? Are these easy or hard to build? Is there a risk associated with the process?

    3. Does your organization already do business with similar accounts? What were the issues faced in the early stages of getting that business?

    4. Do you have the necessary connections within the account to identify potential pitfalls?

    5. Do you see any reasons why this account might decide to go another way? What are you doing to address these before you begin?

- Are there any signs of price driven, bargain shopping at the customer? Have they negotiated deals with others which indicate a heavy handed approach to price?

- Does this customer have the proper credit rating with your company to increase business without running into credit hassles? Who handles the credit in your company? Have you talked with them about your choices for strategic customer planning?

Part 8
Following the Money

In an earlier section, we talked about understanding the opportunity presented by an account. Let's push the thought further along. Way back in the late 70s, there was a movie called *All the President's Men* that popularized the catch-phrase, "follow the money." And while the movie put a negative stench on the phrase, for sales types it comes with an especially attractive connotation; like an extra day at the beach with the kiddos or the new car smell. So with this thought, hop in, buckle up and join me as we... follow the money.

Most sales people study technology, assist with applications, explore customer needs and pursue friendly yet mostly "technical" contacts; they don't follow the funds. I can't help but wonder if a lot of sellers actually feel their work is somehow compromised by the exchange of money. How many times you have heard a salesperson lament:
"The proposal was perfect. The product was everything the customer wanted. We are the best supplier on the planet. But, the customer's top brass 'nixed it' because they didn't have any funding."

Think about this for a moment. Selling time, pre-sale research, product specialists, engineering resources and a ton of money spins and swirls its way down the proverbial drain. It all could have been avoided by asking a couple of well selected questions/phrases.

Here are six easy examples:
1. How does your company justify projects like this one?

2. Does the whole thing go through a process or committee for final approval?

3. What kind of budget do you have for something like this? I want to make sure you get the best deal for your money and understanding the budget helps me focus our work.

4. What are the financial issues driving this decision? I want to better understand how the need for improvements are discovered.

5. What kind of payback is required to make this project work? Is there anything I need to provide you for the analysis?

6. Who holds the purse strings for a purchase like this in your company, maintenance, production, engineering or somebody else?

In an earlier part of our discussion around building a customer based strategic plan, we spoke about our need to fully understand the value provided to the customer. Following the money is only partially financial in nature. By focusing attention away from the "stuff" in our catalog and onto the inner workings of the customer, we segregate ourselves from the unclean hordes of drive-by salesmen.

Without overtly thinking about making a change, we shift from a guy with products for sale to a trusted advisor. Since most companies (like our customers) exist to produce revenue, partners who understand how to help them make more money are esteemed partners.

An aside from the author:
This is for those of you who were forced to study Shakespeare as a teenager. Miss Miller, my 8th grade English teacher, called this section a soliloquy. I don't write many but here goes...
I know your products are spectacularly interesting; they probably have the latest "double-dip-thong" technical wizardry. My guess is your company has a really creative Vision Statement and a trip through your warehouse is like a visit to the NASA's Top Secret Space Lab. But, all of this is only mildly interesting to your customer contacts. If the contact happens to be a financial guy (Plant Manager, VP of Operations, Production Manager or somebody else), your product selling scoop bores them to tears. They only want to talk about their company and money. Period!

That Ladies and Gentlemen is how a soliloquy works. Now back to Part 8 already in progress.

Understanding funding issues is not only important to your credibility, but it gives you some old-fashioned selling advantages as well.

We must anticipate the money.
Salespeople who know "where the money comes from" are able to anticipate its arrival. Fully understanding the drivers behind a potential project before the competition hears about it is a powerful strategic advantage. The salesperson who anticipates the coming "money" can build credibility with people they may have missed in normal/routine sales calls to the customer. These informed sellers can better research new product or technology advantages to the customer. By gathering more information and reinforcing their company's service, they outperform less prepared competitors. Prepared sellers discover insider information which makes their proposals ring true to the customer. When a proposal references specific customer trouble spots rather than the generic issues of an industry, the customer finds themselves nodding along in agreement. This is a major step in the buying process.

On a non-customer level, distributors with non-exclusive suppliers can use the extra time to lock in on special pricing agreements, strengthen relationships with the supplier and leverage the information with the supplier to build a cost-based competitive advantage.

Do you know everybody?
Money discussions flush out new people at the customer. While most sellers have keen awareness of those in engineering, project management, maintenance and similar positions, most find it difficult to constantly search for those with indirect influence. To illustrate the point, allow me to provide an example from the automaton world.

OSHA regulations put into effect require companies with robotic and metal forming equipment to install safety equipment designed to keep workers away from danger. Distributors serving the industry are well versed in the equipment required to provide the protection. They are respected by automation professionals working at their customers. However, very few of these distributors cultivate relationships with safety managers. Why? Most safety professionals come from non-technical Human Resources (HR) backgrounds, so conversations on the technology are mostly beyond the comprehension of the safety department personnel. Sellers assumed their technical counterparts would bring them into selling situations when appropriate. But, there was a breakdown.

First, many of the engineering types didn't fully understand the scope of the OSHA regulations. Because many of the pieces of equipment had been in operation for years with few safety incidents, they assumed the regulations either did not apply or were unwarranted. Safety managers sought help from new suppliers, often specialists marketing directly to safety departments. Because safety groups controlled the budget, the new suppliers had a distinct competitive advantage. Orders were lost, new competitors introduced and, in hindsight, the whole situation could have been prevented by following the money.

Saving time and effort.
Have you ever worked long hours diligently creating a detailed quotation based on the feedback of one of your customers only to be told, they really only wanted a "ball park" price to determine future funding. What if you knew the person controlling the budget? What if you could have simply walked your way through a couple of similar projects done by your organization and put together a five minute response to help steer financial folks in understanding the payback of the project?

Time and again, experience indicates, the technical folks we deal with on a daily basis don't understand all of the criteria for justifying a coming project. As strange as this scenario sounds, it continues to surface on a regular basis. In addition, understanding the justification behind the finances, allows the seller to understand the importance of the project to the financial person figuratively "signing the check." Remember, projects which are low risk and high reward call for more effort than their low payback brethren.

Short circuit purchasing/procurement based negotiations.
Allow me a moment to stereotype. Working under the black flag of "Buy the best solution on the planet, for the price of a sloppy second rate hack job," purchasing people exist to drive your price down (and summarily, take money from you and your employer). Understanding the finances gives you the opportunity to negotiate from a position of strength. Allow me to share and example.

I was asked to help a machine builder negotiate the contract for one of their machines. After detailed discussions with the president of the customer, we clearly understood the machine builder's unique position to provide exactly the kind of solution the customer needed. Based on the original "book" price, the president said, "This is exactly what we need and I will ask our purchasing department to send you an order." It was 10:00 AM. We boarded a plane and were out of touch for two hours. When we landed, my client's phone had a message from the customer's purchasing manager. We assumed it was an order confirmation or questions about purchase order minutia. It wasn't.

The purchasing guy came on with a message indicating that several other companies had similar or better solutions but he would let us have the order if we could just find a way to trim $50,000 off of the price. A quick call back to the company president indicated he was both excited to get the machine and wanted to see if we might expedite its delivery date. The purchasing comment just didn't sound right.

Waiting till near the end of the working day, we called the purchasing department. My machine builder friend told the procurement guy, we had slotted a start date and were ready to get started. He tossed out, "So you can drop the price for me?" I can only imagine the look on his face when he heard that his president had told us he wanted the machine and wanted it soon; at the original price. He muttered, "It's my job to ask." and immediately faxed the order confirmation. I could recite other examples but it pays to know where the money comes from and why.

Thinking a little more about money.
There are a half dozen other advantages to following the money. Many of these involve nuances in managing your business; things like inventory and staffing. But from a purely selfish selling standpoint, imagine the time advantage of knowing the difference between funded spending and a pie in the sky chase down a rabbit hole. Time is the world's first unrenewable commodity. There will be times when something has to be pushed aside. Why not put off the unfunded sale?

Pushing forward...

In Part Nine, we will explore how to engage suppliers and vendors in the strategic plan. Because distributors serve as the middle-man between supplier and customer it is imperative that, in the best of situations, we enlist their aid in completing the plan and at least, position our efforts to block out competitors or other distractions to the plan.

Points to Ponder:

- Talk to the CFO of your own company and ask how capital projects are evaluated. Understand how it works within your own organization as a background for your exploration at customers.

- Think about how you can smoothly broach the subject with customers. Think of your own set of questions similar to the half dozen presented early in this section.

- Revisit a project which was not implemented because of lack of funding. Ask someone at your customer to help you understand why the project was not set in place? If the contact you are speaking to uses vague terms, ask for specifics as to who makes the decision or how decisions like that are made. If the person can't tell explain it, you need to ask someone else.

- Do you know the payback required to make a project viable at your customer? Typically these are measured by months or years. Generally, during good times projects with a payback under a year are considered worthy of pursuing?

- Set up a management to management meeting to explore the future direction of the customer. During this meeting ask your manager to ask about how capital investments are evaluated.

Part Nine – Partners, Allies, Friends and Money

No man is an island, it takes a village; heck the Lone Ranger had Tonto, Bevis has Butt-head and, stretching things to the limit of reason, Ren, the insanely psychotic Chihuahua plays off a dimwitted cat sidekick named "Stimpy" (Stimpson J. Cat). There is power in teams.

We've discovered in today's selling environment most salespeople work as part of a team. While the structure of the team varies based on the industry, organization and technologies sold, the basic framework is almost always the same. The salesperson acts as the leader orchestrating longer term strategy and individual tactical moves. When it works, the beauty of the concept brings a tear to my eye. On the flip side, a dysfunctional team is a train wreck looking for a place to happen.

We are going to break this subject into two sections.
- Other employees from within your own organization

- Supply-partners and various vendors

While each category is part of the salesperson's team, the groups rarely behave the same and often need a different bit of thought to engage them into an account-centric strategic plan.

Allow me to quickly digress and remind you, we are engaged in strategic planning for individual accounts. For the sake of brevity, we'll skip over the warm and fuzzy rich personal reward of developing a team, fast forward past the psycho-babble of humans being tribal beings and get straight to how we can grow specific accounts by focusing a group of people toward achieving results.

Others from within your organization play a part.
This diverse group can consist of inside sales people, crib specialists, customer service reps, product specialists and delivery drivers, and extends all the way to managers and owners. They all have defined roles in your company, they are probably pretty busy. But in building a strategic plan, you determine how they might be leveraged to bolster your position.

Let's remember: they are already busy, you are busy. Here I go with a rant you've heard/read countless times - sorry. We can't do this for every account; time just doesn't allow it. Instead, we must determine a select few accounts - Accounts where our efforts can make the greatest difference. We are targeting and sharply focusing efforts. Pick too many and the focus is lost. Selecting the targets is entirely your responsibility.

Share the accounts covered by a strategic plan with your co-workers. Connecting your team to your plans for the future achieves three things. First, it allows them to provide feedback from a different point of view. The team may recognize an important point that you missed. Secondly, they can often provide a second (third, fourth...) set of eyes. They may see opportunities, hear about competitive activity or learn of new technology shifts during their normal course of business. Lastly, they may be a key ingredient in moving the opportunity forward. You want them to understand the nature and steps of your account-centric strategic plan.

Of special note is the need for management buy in. If you work for a progressive company, there is a good chance management will be all over the concept of driving individualized strategic plans at critical top target account. If not, you may need to carefully lay out your plan including the need for the use of occasional special resources from the rest of your team. We feel this is so important that we will devote a future chapter (Part Ten) to the topic. For now, make sure you have this critical base covered.

Schedule regular updates on the progress of your plan. The plan belongs to you. Because, you think about it regularly, it's top of mind. You review progress, fine tune activities and heed changes in customer direction. This is likely not the case for your team. It's your job as the plan's owner and champion to regularly review progress, special events and needs for timely support from the group.

We like plans which detail activities with descriptions of the outcome and time lines. Sharing a mutual calendar for the account allows all those involved to fit required actions into their own schedule. If you have the ability to share a flow chart of the actions that's all the better.

A best practice of working with a team comes via the some sort of "huddle session" where everyone gathers to talk about the plan. Typically, these can be done in a few minutes before normal sales meetings. These meetings need not be long or complicated but a quick agenda and notes shared by the salesperson typically pay off by reinforcing the difference between this meeting and the typical account banter which generally takes place. Experience dictates a little formality pulls people further into the process.

Supply Partners and Vendors play a role.
For seasoned distributor salespeople this part should be intuitive, but often it is overlooked so let me explain. Typically, your products and services are not developed, manufactured or delivered exclusively by your company. Supplier sales teams don't work for your organization, but they have a vested interest in the outcome. Your success becomes their success, maybe. It depends on how you handle the situation.

A note from the author: Throughout this section I will refer to supply-partners and vendors as if they were synonyms. I believe there is a difference. Supply-partners see your success as an extension of their own and are more likely to take part in these plans. Vendors on the other hand just allow you to resell their products and services. Think about the difference but test the vendors; some of them may be willing to take part in your plan.

For the next few moments let's frame the situation. The supply-partner gains if you bring them new business. Moving business from one channel, group or department to another creates little, if any, value. Similarly, unauthorized sales of products brought in from another territory will not bring warmth to the local vendor sale guy's heart (because they aren't paid or evaluated on the sale).

The new business snatched from the grasp of a hated competitor is an all-around good deal. Create a new application for their product and they will love you. Solve a problem that locks the supply-partner into the customer forever and you will be a hero.

The important point is this: you have to add some value to the vendor's effort to pull them into your plan. With these points well understood, we can stroll through pulling these people into our strategic plan.

Distributors must reverse sell to vendors.
Unlike members of your team that work for your organization, these folks often must be sold on the value you can provide. This is especially true if your organization is not their favorite partner in the market place.

Information sharing is critical to gaining buy in from this group. Unlike your own team where there is no need to outline "what's in it for them", this group (your Supply-partners and Vendors) needs to understand how developing the account can create value for their organization.

Topics to explore might be:
- The strategic importance of the customer to the market served.

- The upside growth for their products if the account can be properly controlled.

- The potential future projects or applications available for their products.

- Competitors currently positioned and the opportunity to replace them.

- Needs for pricing support to push out a competitor.

In a world where we often find multiple channels to market for larger manufacturers, bringing the vendor into your plan actually blocks interference from competing distributors or channels to market. Make sure you cover one important fact. You are about to create value for the supplier and you need to be paid for your efforts; protecting your selling work is critically important.

Once the vendor has shown support for your plan (and not until) outline your longer range strategic plan. Ask how the supplier could assist you. Often, your plan can become part of their own plan. Whenever possible, list specific activities on behalf of the vendor along with completion dates.

When the suppler (especially the case of those with close relationship to you and your company) demonstrates an interest in being part of the total picture, it may make sense to include them in discussions (huddles) with your own internal team.

Leading, Directing, Orchestrating and Managing the activities of others (both groups).
Long ago I had a mentor who often stated:
"As the salesperson, you own the customer. Everybody else has responsibilities that touch up against the customer. They can make a positive impression or they can destroy the customer's potential to buy. When others screw up at your customer, they get chastised. But if the customer is lost, you get 100% of the blame. And because of that, you need to coach, handle, supervise and direct all of the others touching your account. Sometimes, doing such is a contact sport."

Let me confess, these were scary words for a 29 year old guy with a wife, freshly minted mortgage and baby on the way. The list of people touching my customer-base was huge. None of them worked for me. Most of them had more industry experience than I possessed at the time. All that, and I saw that a couple of miss communications could cost me commission dollars, future promotions and maybe even my career if things really crashed. Failure was not an option.

Taking these words to heart, I noticed a few things that worked. Here is my short list:
- The team needs to understand why success is likely. You have already spent a great deal of time understanding the account, gathering data, building alliances with contacts within the account. You are definitely not bringing them into something half-baked and iffy. Your plan is the

"real deal" and they are joining a team with high probability of winning.

- Everyone touching the account needs to know a bit of the "back story", things like customer politics, our current competitive situation and how the opportunity had come into view.

- Any activity assigned to a group of people rarely gets done without some personal intervention. It is always better to ask for one person to complete the task.

- Activities assigned to others need to have dates for completion attached.

- Over communicate. A number of short huddle sessions keeps your team engaged in your plan.

- Avoid long periods without an account update. Sometimes carrying out a real strategic plan takes 10-12 months. Even if no milestones are met or signs of success demonstrated, let the team know the plan is still pushing forward.

- Sometimes, members of your team need to be held accountable for poor performance or lack of follow through. Don't be afraid to speak directly and sometimes, forcefully. Make them understand how their work impacts the whole plan.

- Share success with the group. Make everyone feel like their efforts were critical to the total success. Whenever possible, share the group's success with their boss and coworkers. Public praise goes a long way towards driving participation in future endeavors.

Wrapping all this up...
Building a team accelerates your success. Time is a resource; one that cannot be replenished. Pulling others into your plan multiplies your time. Further, teams built for one account can quickly be morphed to address others. Salespeople who pull this off once are seen as the proverbial rain maker. And you are set to share the gains.

Finally, we feel so strongly on the need to actively engage management, that we are devoting a whole section to the top. In Part 10, we'll dig further into putting your boss to work.

Points to Ponder:

- Who in your organization would be a good resource to involve in your strategic plan?

- Who are the trusted Supply-partners you know would be "on board" with your team concept? What makes them different than others (we will call them Vendors)?

- What can you do to prepare your plan to include Vendors (who may have other distributors working in your territory)?

- Is your customer already making purchases from a Vendor through another distributor? Do you have a plan for dislodging the incumbent distributor?

- Are Special Pricing Agreements (SPAs) part of the landscape in your industry? If so, have you talked to your Supply-partners and Vendors about the opportunity to establish an SPA for your account?

Part Ten – Getting Management Involved

Most of the time, we work for them, but strategy minded salespeople have learned how to turn the table and put the boss to work at their accounts. If you can get your boss involved, you win. Why? Because they have the power to approve strategic low margin sales (not that I would ever want you whistling the tune of AC/DC's Dirty Deals Done Dirt Cheap) but sometimes it's needed to kick start something big. Your boss may have a membership at some cool country club and your customer likes to play golf, that's a door opener too. And finally, your boss might be able to better relate to the owner of one of your accounts better than you – age, business experience, or any of a hundred other reasons.

Finally, with tongue firmly planted to cheek, you might go for the sympathy purchase. Your boss might be such a Type A jerk that customers will throw down purchase orders just to show sympathy for your work-life balance. It worked for me, once.

The nitty gritty of putting your boss to work.
It was the age of leisure suits and wingtips. Sales offices were richly appointed in thickly shagged carpet and orange metallic furniture. The computer, fax machine, Internet, smartphone, tablet and text message were years away. Actually, the latest bit of sales technology centered on the auto-flip Rolodex. Times were different; very different. To further amuse our younger readers, a couple of decades ago, distributor owners and sales managers spent significant time visiting customers and traveling with their salespeople. It was the management style of the day.

Today, distributors cover more products and larger geographical territories, and the business is more complex. Back in simpler times, value propositions centered on accurate billing, local inventory and easy credit terms. Value-adds had yet to enter the lexicon of distributors. Solution selling requiring qualified support staff, product specialists and expensive product demo laboratories was totally unheard of. Distractions created by emails and supplier-driven reports were years away.

In these "olden days" distributor owners and their management staff were far more tuned into customer personalities and reinforcing relationships. While I have seen very convincing arguments for a return to the "good old days" of customer connection, distributors today face a whole different set of challenges. Actually, I doubt if returning to the old ways is even possible. The typical distributor sales manager lacks the bandwidth to even begin approaching the issue.

All this being said, I believe successful sellers still make good use of their boss as a strategically important sales tool. Let's outline the best practices of utilizing management to accelerate sales growth.

It's the seller's Job to manage leadership. Really.
We started the discussion off with what one client calls (tongue firmly planted in cheek) "bring your boss to work day." Salespeople must think of their management team as a powerful resource they can channel for growth. With this thought, I believe it is the responsibility of the seller to determine the right place to activate and engage their company's leadership team. I don't believe management should be responsible for setting up the call or even proactively pushing their sales team to arrange a call. The truth is, most of the time they are too busy. Instead, for all but the newest salesperson, the onus of determining the right customer and scheduling the interaction falls on the strategic-thinking seller.

Like all good joint calls, the purpose of the call, the personalities involved and inter-call scripting are details established well ahead of the actual interaction. Follow-ups must be discussed and planned out immediately following the visit; with dates and milestones for completion established. The salesperson retains the responsibility for insuring actions are finished within the customer's time frame and expectations. With this in mind, let's look into some of the best uses of the distributor leadership.

Don't wait until a fiasco to show commitment.
Sadly, industry observations point out the most common management-customer interaction occurs during some major customer flare-up. Here's an often-seen scenario: A supplier misses a delivery date, the customer's project is massively delayed, tempers flare, the "legal beagles" growl, and the management team "gets to" meet the customer. With hat in hand and a pocket full of sales concessions, distributor leadership rushes in for damage control. Wouldn't it have been nice if this wasn't their first meeting?

Imagine a different scenario. Here the distributor's salesperson makes the effort to arrange an annual meeting between someone on the leadership team and key customer personnel at carefully selected strategic accounts. Call it a customer strategy review, value meeting or something of your own choosing, but make it happen. And while going to the trouble, ensure the meeting is meaningful; not just a firm handshake and a couple of flowery words followed by golf.

Boss meets customer meeting ideas.
Make the meeting strategically important by providing insight to your mutual work together and by establishing a dialog for mutual growth. Consider these topics:
- Statistics on orders placed, deliveries made, product types purchased and seasonal sales trends.

On the surface, this topic seems duller than paint drying, but it offers a vehicle for you and the boss to expound on local support inventory, emergency deliveries, order fill rates and your company's unique ability to support the customer during the off-season.

- The meeting might restate and reaffirm customer value created throughout the year.

Call it value-add, specific customer value metrics or something flowery your boss likes, but taking time to outline examples of the work you have done to benefit the customer is a best practice. Whenever possible, the boss should use numbers provided to you by various customer contacts throughout the year. One example might be, "Your operations manager Bruce tells us our shift to 7 a.m. deliveries saves more than three trips back to the shop every day. With time and mileage thrown in, we believe your savings of $20,000 a year justifies the overtime spent in our warehouse."

- New programs soon to be released from your organization make for good discussion.

Why not allow the boss to present new programs on the horizon with your organization? This gives the customer an opportunity to provide feedback and serves to strengthen your ability to negotiate minor changes to the program to benefit your customer (and further lock in sales).

- Why not gather the customer's opinion on new product offerings?

With distributors migrating into new technologies, new supply partners and adjoining lines of trade, I can't imagine a distributor where this is not a good topic of discussion. Having someone from the leadership of your company solicit opinions enhances the customer relationship by allowing them a mechanism to "buy into" your future offering.

- The big kahuna, the R&D of distribution.

Manufacturers have R&D departments scanning the horizon for new product opportunities and exciting customer trends. For most distributors, the best R&D comes directly from customers. Imagine the response if your boss said this: "As a distributor, we don't have an R&D department, our only research involves our customers. It isn't enough for us to provide you with products and services now. We have to be ready for your future needs. And it takes time to prepare. Can you give us just a short review of how you believe your business will change in the coming years and how you see your needs changing?"

Use your boss to move up in the organization.
As strange as it may seem, many distributor salespeople don't enjoy good relationships with the real power people at their accounts. They justify their lack of connection with a number of excuses. Many believe their project or service manager buddy carries the real buying clout. But, over the years, a host of great distributors have found themselves on the outs because a competitor nurtured a relationship at the top. Some worry a quality call on the customer's top management might damage the relationship with current contacts. Here is where the boss can help.

Why not leverage a call with the boss to meet and further your company's relationship with the financial leaders at your customer? If you use some of the strategies outlined above, invite your customer's top brass. If you have yet to set up a review meeting, launch the call with something to the effect of, "Mr. Big, your company is one of our major clients. I would like to introduce you to my boss so that he might learn a little more about your organization. This will not be a sales call. Instead, we want to learn how we might be able to serve you more effectively."

Offering up advanced business solutions.
One of the results of the various meetings we've outlined could be ideas for non-product business solutions. Engaging the clout of your leadership team speeds the process and allows for more meaningful give and take during the discussions.

Examples of advanced business solutions might include any of the following: Inventory management, service truck stock programs, job trailers, consigned inventory, summary billing and more progressive payment terms. In every case, management level participation makes your job as a salesperson easier and speeds up the process.

Keys to working with the boss.
As you lay plans to "bring your boss to work," there are a few points to remember. The relationship with the account belongs to you. Even if the boss is responsible for screwing something up, it's your mess to clean up. In every case outlined above, the seller must accept responsibility for not only planning the activity but also the content. Research, homework as well as legwork are required.

In nearly every case, the salesperson will need to spend time well ahead of the appointment to gather data, develop presentations, lay out scripts and set expectations. Consider this part of the bargain. Your leadership team is a powerful tool to drive business forward. They have a vested interest in seeing your business grow. Driving their involvement will ultimately accelerate your success.

One last thought on using your leadership team.
If you are a salesperson reading this, engaging your management team at your accounts can open the doors to more than just bigger sales and larger commission checks. Demonstrating your ability to think strategically demonstrates your ability to lead people. Whether you work for a bigger company or a small family owned business, this creates extra career opportunities.

Stretching further, let's say you are someone who just doesn't like to be micromanaged by your boss. Bringing in your boss creates a management mindset that you are someone your management doesn't really need to manage because you openly bring them in when the situation is right. You get additional freedom and the personal reward of being put above the rest of the pack.

For sales managers and other leaders, encouraging your people to follow these guidelines takes away from concerns you might have as to what's going on at important accounts. In addition, this process puts the burden of setting schedules and determining the right conversation onto the person responsible for the account – the salesperson. It's a win-win deal.

Thinking strategically...
We have covered ten major topics in developing a strategic plan for your accounts. Individually, each of them give you tools for accelerating sales growth, but the real strength comes when you lay them over the top of each other to build a solid plan for the future. I would encourage you to systematically apply each in the order they have been presented.

Points to Ponder:

- Let's take inventory. Who does your leadership team know at your strategic accounts? This might include previous business relationships, social connections and acquaintances made via local business groups.

- Who in your leadership team could be useful in your work? While most people automatically think about their sales manager, experience dictates the President, CFO, COO and others are valuable in moving strategic plans forward.

- Thinking about your best strategic customer, what are some of the topics you might use your leadership team to bridge?

- At which of your strategic accounts do you seriously lack in the "management connection" department? How might you use your leadership team to begin building a relationship?

There's Never a Real End to Strategic Thinking, but...

Because most people never have the opportunity to write a book, I thought I would give you some insight into the process. This journey came out of real situations with hundreds of salespeople; some were neophytes, others were experienced folks with a respectable level of success. While reviewing notes from our interactions, we discovered only a few had developed the ability to disconnect from their daily activities and think about customers in a strategic way.

In the rare cases where strategic vision was applied to accounts, great things happened. The sellers positioned themselves and their companies not only for the good times, but their efforts were far more rewarding during the turbulence of the last recession. Most experienced some recession driven negativity, but the drop was less profound and the comeback arrived months before the typical salespersons upswing.

As with organizational strategic planning, there are three critical components of a customer driven strategic plan.
1) Understanding your position at the account. Note: this is not for a group of accounts, a territory or even an industry vertical on your account list. It's for one specific account.
2) Analyzing the opportunities with the greatest chance of success will make a huge difference in your performance, today and into the future.
3) Focusing time and effort on accounts capable of providing a return on your sales investment.

I realize I am sounding preachy, but...
Applying these principles to the accounts of a distributor salesperson drives another important point; we can't do this for every account. With

the typical salesperson's limited time and the narrow bandwidth of most distributor managers, it is especially important to gauge which account deserves the extra attention. For most, the object of your attention falls at the top of your account list. Throughout this work, I suggest no more than ten carefully selected accounts. Establishing this behavior provides for both a strong defense of existing business and a powerful offense in taking business from the competition.

Finally, I believe these plans must be reviewed and refreshed regularly. This is not a once and done exercise. However, if you change any of the accounts being focused on, make sure there is a good reason. Further, if you find yourself changing the names on your "strategic account list" frequently, there is a good possibility your logic in selecting the right accounts is flawed.

A personal note from me to you...
If you have troubles along the way, don't be afraid of reaching out. You can call, email or send a reliable carrier pigeon on its way. I enjoy hearing from those on the front lines of distributor sales. It's invigorating and energizing to talk to sales professionals sharpening their skills.

I would like to thank you for spending the time with me. I attempt to write in a conversational tone, that's my approach. Nothing about any of this is complicated so why insert fancy words. Being an engineer by training, I can't help but apply some analytics to everything. Based on my calculations of approximately 24,000 words in this book and an average reading rate of 200 words per minute (assuming you didn't take the Evelyn Woods speed reading course) you've spent something like two hours with me. Thank-you.

If you want to read more...
Allow me to invite you to join "The Distributor Channel Blog" online. We post information with the same straight forward approach there 40-50 times per year.

Signing off from the High Bluffs of the Mighty Mississippi at Davenport, Iowa.

Frank Hurtte

Made in the USA
Middletown, DE
14 May 2021